ANIMAL POWER

ANIMAL POWER

100 ANIMALS TO ENERGIZE YOUR LIFE AND AWAKEN YOUR SOUL

ALYSON CHARLES

Illustrations by
WILLIAN SANTIAGO

CHRONICLE BOOKS
SAN FRANCISCO

Library of Congress Cataloging-in-Publication Data

Names: Charles, Alyson, author. | Santiago, Willian, illustrator.
Title: Animal power : 100 animals to energize your life and awaken your soul / Alyson Charles ; illustrations by Willian Santiago.
Description: San Francisco : Chronicle Books, [2021] | Includes index.
Identifiers: LCCN 2021006236 | ISBN 9781797209531
Subjects: LCSH: Animals–Miscellanea. | Shamanism. | Magic.
Classification: LCC BF1623.A55 C43 2021 | DDC 201/.44–dc23
LC record available at https://lccn.loc.gov/2021006236

Manufactured in China.

Illustrations by Willian Santiago
Design by AJ Hansen and Kristen Hewitt

10 9 8 7 6 5 4 3 2

Chronicle Books LLC
680 Second Street
San Francisco, California 94107
www.chroniclebooks.com

DEDICATION

I dedicate this book to all of the loving guides who came in one day to provide my spiritual awakening.

To Great Spirit and Great Mother Earth for your ever-present guidance, support, and love for my calling and journey.

To the power animal world for coming to me to cocreate this book and trusting me to be a voice for you.

To First Nations for being the first peoples to answer the call of shamanism and for so powerfully keeping sacred wisdom traditions and truths alive.

To my family, friends, and colleagues who have steadfastly supported me and my mission.

To myself for my courage, integrity, passion, love, and willingness.

And to all you brave and bright souls who allow yourselves to awaken your own truth and power through the energy medicine in this book.

CONTENTS

INTRODUCTION

GUIDANCE FOR THE GREAT AWAKENING

AUTHOR'S NOTE

Before we begin, I'd like to share a little about myself and the origins of this book so you can feel the great love, honor, and joy from which it was created.

This book is rooted in shamanism, an ancient spiritual healing art. The word *shaman* is said to derive from the word *saman* (from the Tungusian language of Siberia) and means "one who sees in the dark" or "one who knows."

While the word shaman comes from ancient Siberia, the spiritual path and various forms of shamanism started with the very first peoples of our planet, the peoples of Africa. Various forms of shamanism have been practiced and shared on every continent and in countless cultures throughout human history.

A main function of shamanic energies and medicines is to work with us Earth-inhabiting humans as we each learn to operate from our most aligned, whole, and love-based place. Shamanism heals and connects us with our souls, and the call to shamanism is a soul-level calling. Shamanism is a planetary and inclusive practice; it is the spiritual and energetic truth of the Earth and Universe.

When entered into with reverence, honor, sacredness, and respect, working with shamanic wisdoms to learn and heal is open to anyone inhabiting planet Earth. Its foundational teachings are about oneness, unity, and acceptance.

Answering the very specific soul-level calling to be a shaman—as I have—can be an incredibly challenging, initiatory, miracle-filled pathway. Having the divine call to become a shaman and take full responsibility for this specific way of living, embodying, and teaching is very different than feeling a tug to experience shamanic practices. Both pathway options—the path to exploring, learning, and experiencing shamanic ways and the path to answering a very specific, soul-activated, and true call to be a shaman—move beyond a person's ethnicity, age, or gender and have everything to do with one's soul, reverence, honor, truth, integrity, embodiment, and respect.

There are a lot of deeply ingrained misperceptions about what shamanism is, and popular culture—movies, TV shows, and other forms of entertainment—has sometimes added to the misconception that shamans must look or be a certain way. The media has had a propensity to portray shamanism in ways that aren't divinely true, often sensationalizing shamanism and using its mysteriousness and ancient intrigue to depict it in ways that perpetuate inaccurate understanding. Because of this, shamanism has been pushed into the smallest of boxes. Shamanism is about infinite expansion and evolving into your highest potential, and that tiny, limiting box goes completely against that. It's time for shamanism to be liberated into truth again.

By opening our minds and hearts to these expanded and truth-filled possibilities, we can experience compassion and nonjudgment and avail ourselves to the infinite miracles that shamanism offers.

Shamans walk with feet in both worlds, the seen and unseen. While the shamanism I practice works directly with Great Mother

Earth and Great Spirit, there are also shamanic paths that work with specific lineages rooted in Earth-based traditions. If you are called to work with a specific culture or heritage, it's vital to honor that culture and get permission before sharing any of their specific shamanic teachings. Even if one's shamanic call does not adhere to a specific Earth-based lineage, it is still vital to honor and give back to First Nations and the ancient cultures who were some of the first people to practice shamanic traditions and who carried those teachings and ways for many thousands of years. This book includes stories directly from the mouths of spiritual teachers and shamanic colleagues from around the globe. Some are operating from forms of shamanism similar to mine, and others have taken culturally based paths. All forms are held, unified, and celebrated in this book.

I want to acknowledge that working with power animals can be a sensitive issue. I acknowledge that many shamanic lineages have had to hide their teachings and practices for far too long, and that there have been people who exploited sacred traditions that honor the spiritual relationships between humans and animals. I also acknowledge that I am absolutely in a position of privilege to be among those who are able to share about shamanism publicly. Because of all of that, since my shamanic call awakened, I have tuned in daily with Great Spirit and Great Mother Earth, along with other main spiritual guides in the unseen realms, to ensure I am living in direct alignment with my Earth mission and the precise energies and teachings I am here to share. I have also had countless conversations with shamans all over the world about our practices and what shamanism is. In every one of those conversations, all of us shamans embraced, celebrated, and embodied the same sentiment that because shamanic practices are for the entire planet and infinite Universes, they are for everyone to have the opportunity to explore, learn, and hopefully evolve from.

It is my greatest honor to be entrusted by the animal world to be a voice for them, and it is my greatest honor to be a shaman, to have the courage to answer the specific call to shamanism, and to be entrusted in all of this by Great Spirit and Great Mother Earth.

Being a truly embodied shaman means you completely devote yourself to your wholeness and calling, and in turn, you live by the calls and instructions you are given by Source. I do this work with honor, reverence, and sacredness, and in full alignment with the way my teachings are divinely designed to be shared with the world. For me, working directly with the ancient wisdom within, my heart, God, Goddess, Great Spirit, and Great Mother Earth is vital, and I live in constant surrender, every day, to living in this space.

It is from this divinely guided place that this entire book was created. I had a different book concept in the works, but on a trip to Bali, various animals from the power animal world, which I've worked closely with for many lifetimes, came to me and told me that I was to work with them to write this book. So, *Animal Power* was born.

The purpose of this book is to embody the answering of the divine call and share work that is inclusive, filled with love and unity, and celebrates all beings. This is why *Animal Power* includes a breadth of voices and experiences highlighting the transformational impact that shamanic practices can have in people's lives, no matter where they live.

And in true representation of the universal, inclusive nature of shamanism, there are people in this book sharing their stories from all over the world who work in various shamanic and spiritual traditions. In these pages, we are all coming together to celebrate the rich history of working with power animals with honor as part of a timeless global tradition.

So, welcome to the world of shamanism and the wisdom of the animal realm! I invite you in with open arms and pure love. What new worlds will the transmissions and blessings in this book open to you? Will you be pulled to go deeper into experiencing shamanic traditions? Or is there a soul-level, spiritual, or shamanic-based call that's always been living within you and is ready to be awakened? There are infinite and wondrous possibilities awaiting you inside this very book.

WELCOME TO ANIMAL POWER.

This book will help guide you to the transformation, richness, and unconditional love that your soul is so ready for. In these pages, you will connect with one hundred power animals and discover their energetic medicines, sacred powers, and ability to change your life.

We are here during a time of great awakening on the planet, a new paradigm where many of us feel our souls urging us to be true to ourselves. People are asking more than ever before, "Why am I here, and what is my soul's purpose?" People want to know how they can be of greater service to humanity and the planet. This great awakening brings a lot with it, both externally and internally. Aligning with guidance and support allows our evolution to happen with more ease and grace, two essences that are always highly treasured on the awakening or spiritual path. No matter whether you're just beginning your inward quest or you're a seasoned spiritual warrior, this book is a tool to help you unlock your true and infinite potential by connecting to the sacred power of the animal world.

Power animals have been celebrated in so many ways in so many different cultures. Working with power animals has always been a planetary practice. As you move through this book, you will be immersing in blessed energetic transmissions; ancient animal wisdoms passed on for thousands of years; and eye-opening, soul-expanding teachings, messages, and guidance communicated directly to me from the animals themselves.

Along with each animal's signature powers and energies, I've also included very personal power animal stories and examples from my own life. There are also stories from other well-known voices, spiritual and shamanic teachers and elders from around the world. Together, they illuminate the incredible benefits of working with power animals' healing energies. They share the rich histories and traditions surrounding these beings, and remind us that the animals are our great teachers, worthy of reverence and respect.

The energy medicine and power practices in the following pages are grounded in shamanic wisdom. You can refer to my author's note on page 9 for a more complete explanation of shamanism.

Shamans have the ability to "walk in two worlds," meaning both the seen, physical world and the unseen world, where we are able to connect with and travel to different dimensions, realms, and higher states of consciousness. Many shamans, myself included, can enter unseen worlds on demand or with the use of instruments, plants, and other spiritual tools. When in these different dimensions, we're able to access an infinite amount of information, healing energies, and answers and connect with helping spirits, other-dimensional beings, ascended masters, ancestors, and others who have passed on. The unseen realms are infinite, which allows this work to be forever fascinating and a forever path—the places in which to learn, explore, and connect are truly never-ending.

The purpose of shamanic work is to raise consciousness and love, activate the true divine power of all that is, and be a supportive guide in alleviating suffering. If you are called to work with a shaman, it is vital to listen to your own intuition and soul to ensure that the shaman you select is filled with integrity and love, truly walks the walk, and "feels right" to you.

My initiation into the world of shamanism came many years ago through a divine intervention and simultaneous spiritual awakening. I was in the midst of ending a very toxic long-term relationship and was at the lowest I've ever been. After a period of separation, we were considering reconciling. I was ignoring signs and messages from my own body and soul and spirit helpers, which were all attempting to get me to exit this dysfunctional situation. I was allowing myself to remain in an unhealthy codependent cycle and going against my mission and soul purpose. The divine intervention happened in a moment when I received clear instructions that led me to a discovery about my partner, one that instantly obliterated the shell of ego and veil of denial that had kept me encased in a dysfunctional cycle. Finally, I was clearly able to see the truth about myself, the relationship, and my role in the world.

This experience was so catalytic and powerful that it completely changed who I was in an instant, and from that moment on, I decided to surrender. I called forward the guidance of Great Mother Earth (rock) and Great Spirit (stars, universe, cosmos, unseen realms). These two places continue to be where I work most from as a shaman and became my name, Rock-Star Shaman. I pivoted to a path of being in complete devotion, to living by their calls (messages) and the divine ancient wisdom, love, light, power, and truth that is within me. While living this way eventually aligned me with my calling as a shaman, the very first message all those years ago was for me to have healing sessions with other shamans. It was in that initial work that my core power animal, the black jaguar, revealed itself.

It is important to note that shamanism is a calling, a sacred mission, a gift encoded in one's soul. When your calling activates, there is absolutely no mistaking it, and it then becomes your sacred duty to open up to, unify with, and embody your calling fully. Walking the path of your calling unites you with your soul, which is what allows you to feel the richest fulfillment, experience miracles, and know your true purpose while you're here on Earth.

I uphold my alignment with my calling as a shaman with deepest reverence. I uphold the way my medicine is designed to work in this lifetime with the utmost honor. I uphold my ever-deepening, one-on-one relationship with the power animal world with sacredness. Living my calling is my greatest gift, my sacred existence. The places, people, and experiences I have been taken to, in order to live my truth, have provided a fullness of life and miracles far beyond my imagination.

Rock (Earth) and Star (Spirit) have been my forever and ever-present main shamanic teachers. I have also been blessed to be united with many other renowned global spiritual teachers, and Indigenous and non-Indigenous shamanic leaders and elders. They come from all walks of life, all over the world, from the Maori people of New Zealand to various tribes in the Amazon, the Mayan healers of Guatemala, the Sufi mystics of Israel, the Wixárika peoples of Mexico, the Balians of Bali, and beyond. I have been so fortunate to have been welcomed into countless shamanic global cultures to immerse myself in sacred ceremony, initiations, and the joyous and profound reconnection with my shamanic soul family here on Earth.

My personal shamanic medicines and path work with the macro planes of shamanism. I do not adhere steadfastly and specifically to one shamanic lineage based here on Earth. However, it is absolutely vital to pay complete honor and sacred respect to the First Nations and First Peoples of the planet. They are the original sacred wisdom keepers and medicine carriers. I have spent countless hours in the presence of many of the world's renowned Indigenous spiritual teachers and elders and feel most at home there. Without the preservation of their wisdom, teachings, and traditions, this world could not make it. So, it is from this place of honoring my friends, teachers, and Indigenous families that you will also be fortunate to share in many of their incredibly powerful and personal stories and teachings in this book.

My life and work are dedicated to preserving Indigenous and non-Indigenous sacred wisdom traditions that celebrate global unity and support the Great Awakening. I am here to share shamanism in the way I am designed to, by helping to activate the Eagle/Condor Prophecy (which speaks of a time when the people of the north, represented by the eagle, and the people of the south, represented by the condor, unify to awaken a time of oneness, consciousness, peace, and love) and the truth that we are all one. This beautiful global scope, spanning countless traditions and lineages all over the world, is represented here in this book. The practice of working with healing properties and power energies of animals has taken place on every continent and is truly for everyone, when entered into with reverence, honor, and respect.

In writing this book, I connected every day with our power animal friends, the wisdom within me, Great Mother Earth, and Great Spirit. I then put down on paper the messages and guidance I am called to share with you. I also tuned into ancient wisdoms about each animal that have been passed on for thousands of years. In addition, I drew upon the incredible knowledge shared with me directly from my Indigenous and non-Indigenous spiritual leader friends and family who have so graciously wanted to be part of blessing this magnificent cocreated book.

Throughout this book, I'll mention my website, alysoncharles.com, where you'll find supportive materials and content that will enhance your journey through *Animal Power*, including shamanic journeys, meditations, and additional courses. If you allow yourself to fully immerse in the energies and information both here and available on my website, you will greatly enhance your personal frequency and connection to your soul's wisdom.

At the heart of it, this work is written with the animals and for the animals, for the preservation and honor of ancient sacred truths. It was created for the awakening of a new paradigm of our planet. And for *you*.

Let's begin.

GETTING STARTED

YOUR GUIDE TO WORKING WITH POWER ANIMALS

WHAT IS A POWER ANIMAL?

Every animal, whether an insect, a mammal, an amphibian, or a bird, possesses energetic healing properties, signature traits, empowering teachings, and messages specifically for our benefit. Animals give us strength, guide us through life, remind us of our own internal power, and are our teachers.

And no matter their looks or reputations, each animal is sacred, whether it's a tick or an elephant. When we work with the spirit of an animal—the energetic aspect of the animal—with reverence and respect, we greatly enhance our lives. There are many ways we can access the guidance of power animals: through meditation, conversation, observation, shamanic journeying, sacred rituals, and other practices. In the following pages, I'll guide you through exercises and rituals that will allow you to tap into each animal's energy with integrity, honor, and, oftentimes, a lot of fun.

There are a number of reasons why you would want to activate your sacred relationship with the spiritual attributions of an animal: They guide and heal us through heartbreak, they help us transcend fears and blocks, they open us up to our true power and radiance, they point us in the direction of living our greatest life, and so much more.

There are various ways our soul and power animals attempt to get our attention so we can tune in to the sacred energy of the animal kingdom. Following are some examples.

You are drawn to a particular animal: Perhaps there is an animal you have just always been deeply drawn to or felt a connection with—this is your soul communicating to you (or vice versa, the animal communicating to your soul and getting your attention) that this animal wants to help you or support you in some way; it has a message for you.

All of a sudden, you're noticing a specific animal everywhere: You're hearing stories about a particular animal, then, as you walk into a store, there's a large picture of that same animal, and that night the animal appears in your dreams, and so on. When an animal is trying to be there for you and align with you for your benefit, it will make its presence known. Then, it is up to you to be consciously aware of this and to read about the animal's energetic medicine to see why it's showing up for you.

You are preparing for a new opportunity or experience: Maybe you're about to pitch a big concept to your work colleagues and you want to call in a power animal to be with you in this venture, so you will feel the specific characteristics you want strengthened within yourself and your project. You will locate the power animal who represents these specific traits and call upon that animal to be with you during the pitch, to empower and bless you and the experience.

Or imagine you're trying to finish a big

project, but you feel intense levels of procrastination that have become debilitating. In this scenario, you would call upon kangaroo, rhinoceros, or roadrunner power animal medicine, because in different ways, they remind you that the power is you and the time is now, and they will get energies springing into action. These animals will help release the confines or energetic blocks creating the procrastination and can be your empowering guides as you finish your work.

You are embarking on a spiritual journey: Another very potent and reverent way to engage with a power animal is by doing a meditation or shamanic journey with the specific intent of calling forth the animal that wishes to support you with where you are in life. Or, we all have what I refer to as a "core" power animal that is assigned to us at birth and is with us every moment of our entire life journey. So if you have yet to meet your core power animal, I recommend meeting this animal for the first time through a shamanic journey that is guided by a trusted shaman. You can experience this specific journey with me on my website at alysoncharles.com.

One of the primary aspects of my work as a shaman is guiding people on these journeys either to meet their core power animal or to set a heartfelt intention to go on a shamanic journey and call whichever animal is there, ready to support the person in that intention, to come forth and reveal themselves. During this guided journey, you can ask the animal questions and receive its empowering advice and teachings. You can ask the animal whether there is any energetic medicine it wishes to provide to you, or you can ask the animal to take you somewhere on the journey that will provide additional clarity. Your connection with power animals and your relationship to this aspect of life and spirituality is one that will organically grow with you. Everyone's voyage is unique.

THE RICH HISTORY OF POWER ANIMALS

For many thousands of years, sacred wisdom traditions have deeply honored the medicine and care that power animals provide to us. Mystics, sages, and shamans throughout the world on every continent have recognized how being consciously aware of what animals are presenting, and what healing properties and wisdom they are bringing forth, can greatly inform our decisions and deeply empower and enhance our direction in life.

Take, for example, the Oglala Lakota (Sioux) tribe and the deep connection some of their people have with the elk. They draw upon many lessons regarding love and relationships, learning from the elk's ability to attract a mate with one mating call. They even created an instrument, the love flute, based on this animal's teaching.

Juan Andi Vargas, a shaman of the Indigenous Kichwa peoples in the Ecuadorian Amazon, shares a story about his community's reverence for tigers (page 260).

In both Celtic and Druidic traditions, cows are highly revered. In Celtic tradition, the bull represents strength, fertility, and power. The Druids associate the female cow with the Earth's energy and the bull with the sun's energy.

Hindus look to Lord Ganesh, the elephant-headed god, to remove their obstacles.

The Yawanawá tribe of South America is another example of a group with a deep relationship to the medicine and healing properties of wild animals. *Yawanawá* directly translates to "the people of the wild boar," and their ability to learn from, tap into, and embody the wild boar is expressed in a multitude of ways. One way includes their singing, which I have been honored to be a part of many times. It is filled with the same divine force and power that the wild boar has. The wild boar represents not judging a book by its cover, facing matters head-on, and possessing the ability to be kind, have many friends, and not carry burdens. I feel the medicine embodied in their sacred voice and songs absolutely transmits these properties.

No matter which honoring method or way feels right to you and your soul when it comes to working with power animals, the most important aspect is keeping these most sacred wisdom traditions alive.

Power animals are our helpers, guides, and generous loving beings here to assist us and support our rise. And the more we look at each animal encounter through this lens, the greater and deeper our rapport and connection with the entire animal world grows and, in turn, the more we as an entire planet connect with compassion, wisdom truths, and unconditional love.

Each and every animal possesses beauty, intelligence, and divine power. We are all one, every living being, whether tiny or slimy, a massive ocean mammal, a desert-roaming creature, or a wild soaring bird. Every animal has a spirit within it that has certain wisdoms, empowering energetic medicines, and teachings for us. They are our brothers and sisters and we are their brothers and sisters.

HOW TO CONNECT WITH ANIMAL POWER

There are different ways to connect with and get to know your core power animal and recognize other power animals that are presenting to empower you at different times in your life. The most preferred method is to immerse yourself in a shamanic journey with a trusted shaman. The shaman can either journey on your behalf and tell you the animal who came forth for you, or the shaman can guide the journey and you immerse in it. In the latter case, you would set the intention for your core power animal to come forth and you would meet the animal yourself.

In addition to your core power animal (the animal that is with you from the moment you are born until you pass), there are many other animals that come in and out of your life to assist with what you are experiencing. The power animal will enter in and try to get your attention to give you messages and energetic medicine, but it is of course your job to be consciously aware, to notice that you saw a ladybug five times in forty-eight hours, and to come to this book to read about it and do the power practice.

In my case, right after my spiritual awakening, along with finding out that the black jaguar is my core power animal, I started noticing three other animals continuously showing up for me in ways I couldn't ignore. And they were all rushing in to lovingly support me as I was going through the most trying, traumatic, yet simultaneously miraculous (although it didn't feel that way for a while) time of my life:

Bear: Bear gave me anchored support, that big papa/mama bear energy. When I would meditate or journey, for many months the bear would come sit behind me and I would be able to sit and lean against it and allow myself to completely let go, just surrender and be held. It gave me time to heal and just be, to let someone hold me so I could feel really supported during this scary time.

Deer: Deer kept my heart soft, gentle, and open. The horrifying breakup that caused my intervention and awakening could have been my downfall. But somehow, I spiraled up. My heart shattered, but deer made sure that as it healed, piece by piece, it wouldn't harden, that it would actually open bigger and brighter than ever before, allowing this breakup to alchemize my heart into one of a healer. Ever heard the saying "hurt people hurt people and healed people heal people"? Sacred deer helped turn me into a healer. She tended to my heart relentlessly and many years later actually came back in to play a very pivotal role in aligning me in my now sacred partnership. Deer took me from being unawakened and in a toxic, abusive relationship all the way to becoming healed and sovereign in awakened, sacred partnership. Talk about miracles.

Frog: Frog reminded me that nature, nature, nature would be my saving grace, my secret key to getting through this process. Because frog is all about cleansing, water energy, processing emotions, and renewal, it was my regular message to take nourishing, healing baths filled with crystals and essential oils and to let myself cry and feel all that I needed to. Frog helped clear me—mind, body, spirit, and soul—so I could spring forward from that time in my life to be a completely new person. And I did.

In this guide you will connect with one hundred power animals who came forth to be a part of this book. If you allow yourself to immerse in the energies and information here, you will also greatly enhance your personal vibration and connection to your soul's wisdom. I recommend that you use this guide on a regular basis to continuously return to your truth and the loving support of our incredible Universe.

The most important part of doing this work is to follow your heart and intuitive guidance. If you notice an animal aiming to get your attention, you can say, "I see you, I honor you. Thank you so much for presenting to me. I am so grateful. I am open to receiving the blessings and messages you've come to provide for me today." Then follow your intuition on what to do next. You can close your eyes, place a hand on your heart, and energetically receive, or if you want to keep your eyes open and observe the animal and learn part of what it is communicating from watching, that's great too.

If you are willing to listen, feel, and see the wisdom of power animals, you will develop this whole, rich, and wonderful spiritual practice of uniting with power animals. Here are just some of the ways in which you can connect with or strengthen your bond with a power animal:

Dance: You can dance to honor and/or evoke the energetic powers of the animal. For example, in a tradition of the Indigenous Wixárika (Huichol peoples of Mexico), one of their most important ceremonies pertains to working with the deer power animal and doing the "dance of the deer." In this ceremony, they call upon this most respected animal of their tradition, this animal that they view as their sacred relative, teacher, and guide.

They dance their prayers while also deeply connecting to Great Spirit and Great Mother Earth, all to honor and enrich their relationship with the deer.

Meditation: You can sit in meditation and ask the power animal to come forward and join you in meditation. During this time, you can ask the animal questions or simply speak your prayers to the animal. Perhaps you want them to really help you on that day, so you ask them to be with you in all moments, guiding, blessing, and protecting you. If it's a certain strength you're calling upon—say, strength of heart-led communication and the ability to express yourself—you could call upon whale to join you in this goal.

Shamanic journeying: You can embark on a shamanic journey, which often involves the use of a shamanic drum or rattle, and either have the power animal reveal who will most be of service for you at this time or call upon a specific animal to join you so you can deepen your connection with it (you can find a guided shamanic journey recording on alysoncharles.com).

Awareness: Other times you will simply have an unexpected awareness of a particular animal, through feeling, remembering, seeing a vision in your mind's eye, or one simply arriving in your thoughts. When this happens, it's important to take an honoring moment to acknowledge the power animal that is revealing itself for your benefit. Thank it for showing up, feel into what it wishes to provide you, or ask why it has come forward and what it wants you to know. Also, you should of course reference the animal in this book.

Sacred space: I highly recommend having an altar space in your home. Altars can be simple and small if you prefer. What is important is that you have a space completely dedicated to time spent connecting in prayer to the guides and animals you work with and with yourself. At your altar you can place a few items that evoke your power and truth, such as the feather of a sacred animal you work with, sacred objects from a sacred location you spent time at, or ceremonial tools. I currently have a painting of a hummingbird at the center of my altar.

These are just some of the beautiful possibilities when it comes to the wondrous world of working with the spiritual aspects and energetic medicinal relationships of animals. It is an incredible adventure to have the honor of connecting in this way to the animal world, reconnecting to the deep truth of the oneness of all that is, and remembering that animals are our teachers, guides, and helpers.

HOW TO WORK WITH THIS BOOK

In these pages, you'll discover one hundred power animals, each with its own entry that shares the animal's unique characteristics, healing properties, and messages, followed by a variety of practices and meditations to help you connect with the animal, including:

Energy medicine: The healing and empowering blessings, transmissions, and messages that are provided on an energetic level for those who are open and willing to receive.

Power practices: Rituals, meditations, and other methods that unite you in a reverent way with the power animal world and are specifically designed to awaken and activate the power that lives within you.

These practices are designed so that you can tune in to them whenever you need them, and they require no special materials. My goal is to empower you to access power animals in a reverent way, whenever you need their sacred energy.

You'll also find sidebars sprinkled throughout the book featuring scientific facts, legends from a range of cultures and traditions, and illuminating spiritual stories from my own journey with power animals.

This book is designed for you to engage with it in a number of ways. Turn to these pages when:

1. You feel an animal is trying to get your attention.
2. You want to embody a specific animal trait.
3. You're looking for some inspiration from the Universe. If you are in need of inspiration or wisdom, use this book as a divination tool: Place the book on your lap, then randomly flip and shuffle through the pages until you feel called to stop on a certain page. Open the book to that page to reveal the animal and message you need for that day or clarity around the particular life experience you're going through.
4. You simply need a moment to let some beauty and sacred wisdom fill your heart.

GLOSSARY OF TERMS

Astral travel: The ability to travel our consciousness to unseen realms and dimensions.

Aura: An energy field that emanates from a living being; a luminous radiation.

Chakra: Energy centers held within and outside of the physical body that when open and functioning healthily, aid greatly in mind-body-soul connection, consciousness rising, and the ability to expand in spiritual awareness. The word *chakra* means "wheel" in Sanskrit, and the concept is believed to have originated in ancient Hinduism.

Energy medicine: The healing and empowering blessings, transmissions, and messages that are provided on an energetic level for those who are open and willing to receive.

Great Spirit: The pure and unconditionally loving creator of all that is.

Kundalini: Rooted in Hindu teachings, Kundalini is the yogic life force that lies coiled at the base of the spine until it is roused and sent to the head to trigger enlightenment.

Medicine traits: Each animal holds unique spiritual abilities and energy. These are their medicine traits. Understanding an animal's medicine traits allows you to work with them as a power animal.

Personal medicine: Each of us carries within us our own unique spiritual energy and blueprint that holds within it ancient wisdom we've carried from past lives; the divine wisdom of what our calling is in this lifetime; specific spiritual gifts and abilities to be of service with; and the way we are designed to carry and express light in order to assist others in returning to their truths and the planet in birthing a new energy field that allows for greater oneness, unconditional love, and unity.

Shadow work: Facing, tending to, and healing aspects of ourselves that operate from places of unresolved trauma, distortion, or dysfunction. Unless consciously faced and examined, our shadow aspects—which emerge as difficult and shameful behaviors or patterns—can rule our lives from our unconscious or subconscious. Doing shadow work allows us to heal and unconditionally love all aspects of ourselves, which allows us to be in our whole power.

Source (also known as Source Consciousness): The place where we tune in to receive divine guidance and information in infinite shapes and forms.

Transmutation: Transmutation occurs when experiences of hardship become growth lessons for your soul. When something is transmuted, a challenging situation becomes a teaching that allows for a positive evolution in your life experience. For example, "She was able to transmute the pain of her breakup and emerge from the experience with greater self-honor and a healthier lifestyle."

Let's now enter the power animal world and connect.

ANIMAL POWER

100 ANIMALS TO ENERGIZE YOUR SPIRIT AND AWAKEN YOUR SOUL

ALLIGATOR

KEEN OBSERVATION • CONSERVING POWER • DIVINE TIMING • MAGIC • TRUTH • CLARITY

WHEN TO WORK WITH ME:

When you are ready to let yourself see truth, when you want clarity on whether to pause or act, when you want to further develop your spiritual gifts and abilities, when you want to evoke magic and miracles

ENERGY MEDICINE:

I observe deeply, sensing, feeling, knowing when it is my time to burst forward with energy.

I use water medicine to keep me calm; it is my safe haven, my solace, my true home.

I bring you keen, focused manifestation—when I become aware of my goal, my vision, and know it is the right time, I go for it with all power, all efforts, all might.

I am a magic wisdom keeper, knower of magic as prehistoric as the beginning of Earth's time.

My great brothers and sisters are the dragons, who share with me the secrets of the Universe.

When I appear for you, it is a sacred time for you to allow the magical medicine that lives within your chakras, blood, and bones to come alive.

Resilience. Patience. Ancient survival. Protection. Call upon me when you want fierce and true awareness of what is for you and not for you and when you want your divine energy field protected from anything that is not love.

I represent intuition and sixth sense. Slow down and feel. Close your eyes, go within, feel the energy in your skin, and ask yourself whether it is time for you, whether that thing is right for you. Let yourself be aware of truth, truth that will ultimately guide you to your greatest thriving and joy.

POWER PRACTICE:

In this visualization practice, you'll tune in to alligator's energy for truth and clarity. Find a quiet place to sit and close your eyes. Inhale through your nose and direct the breaths into the middle of your chest, your heart center. Exhale gently through a slightly open mouth, allowing any areas of tightness in your body to relax. Flow with this breath until you are calm and present. Say inwardly or out loud, "Dear alligator, I invite you to come forth to me." With eyes closed, visualize an alligator walking toward you as your eyes connect with one another. Take a moment with this beautiful and powerful connection. Feel it. Once connection has been established, allow your hands to gently rub over the scales of the alligator's back, feeling the texture. Imagine the alligator inviting you to lie down along its spine, placing your back on its back. Completely release and relax onto the back of the alligator and allow it to carry you, letting it take you where you need to go. As you move with this sacred animal, ask the alligator a question that you need clarity on. Then fully receive its answer. Trust it to guide you to the truth. When your time with the alligator is finished, move off its back, honor it by looking into its eyes, and thank it for showing up for you. Rub your hands along your skin a bit, to get back into your physical body, and then gently open your eyes.

STILLNESS TO SPEED

Despite its short legs, an alligator can climb trees and go from being completely still, to reaching 35 miles [56 km] per hour on land in the blink of an eye. This ability to go from stillness to speed makes it the perfect animal to look to for energetic inspiration when you feel called to action.

ANT

PERSISTENCE • GROUP POWER • DETERMINATION
SMART STRATEGY • HUMILITY • PATIENCE • FOCUS

WHEN TO WORK WITH ME:

When you want to get into alignment with your goals and dreams, when you're ready to do what's needed to serve the greater good, when you need more patience and trust, when you want to hone in on a clear strategy, when you're working with a team or community

ENERGY MEDICINE:

I'm here to activate the powers of keen focus and fortitude within you so you can reach your goals.

Is your ego getting in your way? Are you willing to be more flexible, humble, and cooperative? Think now of a group or family initiative that can reach greater success if stubbornness is released.

I remind you that big dreams sometimes take time to fully manifest. Are you willing to play the long game and steadfastly move toward what you want, no matter the duration?

Do you believe you truly have the power to create the life of your dreams? Are you getting in your own way or sabotaging opportunities that are presenting? Answering these questions will clear the path between you and your goals.

A strong foundation is key for lasting success. Remember that staying in alignment with your integrity and truth, as well as the divine plans of Great Spirit and Great Mother Earth, are always worth it.

I bring you unwavering determination and persistence. Call upon me to help keep you strongly connected with the divine flow of the Universe that will serve the greatest good.

POWER PRACTICE:

In this manifestation practice, you'll work with ant energy to achieve alignment so you can achieve your goals. Collect your journal and a writing implement, and find a quiet place to sit. Close your eyes and connect with your heart and breath. Imagine a line of ants, each one in alignment with the one behind it and in front of it, all working toward a common goal. Holding this image of ants, ask yourself, "My heart and soul—what goal am I ready to manifest?" In your journal, write your goal at the bottom of the page. At the top of the page, make an "X" to represent where you are now. Now, in a line going from the "X" at the top to the goal at the bottom, make a list of the reasons you want this goal, the emotions you want to feel, and the actions you need to take in order to achieve this goal. Each word is an ant, working together to manifest your dreams. Refer to this page daily to find alignment and bring your goal into existence.

ARMADILLO

ENERGETIC ARMOR AND PROTECTION • SELF-WORTH • HEALTHY BOUNDARIES • INDEPENDENCE

WHEN TO WORK WITH ME:

When you want to establish healthy boundaries, when you want to claim independence, when you want to respect yourself and be respected by others, when you want to heal people-pleasing tendencies, when you want to stay in your power

ENERGY MEDICINE:

Are you allowing others to pressure you into a way of being that may not feel aligned with your truth, or are you clear in who you are and able to express that in a healthy way?

I am a most powerful reminder to set boundaries for yourself that honor your needs at this time and to be respectful of others' boundaries too.

If you have experienced any codependent cords in relationships, call upon my medicine shield to sever the ties and support you in moving forward, liberated and free.

If you had to, do you trust that you could make it on your own? Do you believe in your abilities to soar solo through a goal, a project, or even life and be able to thrive?

There is such a thing as convincing yourself you're riding solo for a good reason, when in actuality you're unconsciously trying to shield yourself from experiencing hurt. It's vital to know when to have your guard up and when it's safe to put it down and let love in.

Self-reliance and self-trust are main medicines of mine, but do not venture into isolation for so long that you become lonely or sad due to lack of human connection. Where are you with this?

POWER PRACTICE:

One of armadillo's main medicines is using its shell as a shield, so in this practice, you will work with energetic protection and power. Get your journal and, to the best of your ability, draw an outline of an armadillo with an especially large shell. Next, within the armadillo, write down the things that make you feel powerful. Ask yourself, "What practices activate my power? What activities amplify my power? What emotions make me feel in my power?" And so on. Write at least ten things down. When you've finished, call upon the energetic medicine of armadillo to bless and protect this list for you so that these qualities can appear in your life in abundance. Finish the practice by saying, "And so it is."

ARMORED PROTECTOR

Reinforcing its gift at setting up an energetic shield of protection, the word *armadillo* means "the little armored one" in Spanish. One powerful way to work with the healing and energetic medicines of an animal is to incorporate a piece of the animal—like a feather, a bone, or a shell—into a sacred ceremony. I experienced this when a medicine man from Peru played a *chanrango* during a sound healing ceremony I attended. The chanrango is a small guitar with a resonator made from the shell of an armadillo, rather than wood.

BAT

REBIRTH • MIRACULOUS LIBERATION • TRANSMUTATION • CHANGE

WHEN TO WORK WITH ME:

When you're moving through big life transitions, when you're facing your darkest fears, when your soul knows it's time to go deeper inward than ever before, when you're ready to place the greatest trust in self and the Universe

ENERGY MEDICINE:

I represent rebirth. I am change. I am transformation.

I very powerfully, yet deeply and lovingly, show you how to enter the caves that hold your fears (sometimes greatest fears). Through divine alchemy—the process of facing these fears—you can transcend and rise above them and dislodge any power they once held over you. This process provides deep freedom and anchoring into true self-confidence, self-worth, and self-esteem.

I open up your senses, letting aspects of them that have previously lain dormant come alive. This opening allows you to be more fully connected with yourself, other humans, and the world around you.

I am not to be feared. I am deep and brave love. My potent medicine lets you truly transcend worlds within yourself, which translates to transcending and upleveling in your external existence too.

Especially on the walk of a mystic, shaman, or someone on the hero's journey, my medicine can test you in great ways, helping old parts of yourself not serving your highest, greatest good to die off. You can then come through the portal as more your whole self.

Listen deeply. Pause and feel the air, and hear the whispers of your heart—these are your guides right now. What do they say?

POWER PRACTICE:

Periods of change or difficult transitions offer you the opportunity to tune in to your personal power so that you can rise above the chaos. In this practice, you will connect to bat, known for its agility, along with its ability to recover stability very quickly *and* land upside down. This is a deep and powerful practice where you'll learn to prevent fearful thoughts from consuming you.

Find a place to lie comfortably, either outside on the earth or on the floor. Take a moment to ground yourself by releasing any anxiety or fear into Great Mother Earth and know that you are safe and held. Focus on the area(s) of your life that are changing right now and breathe into your heart the knowingness that these changes are *serving* you. Repeat, "I am safe and held by the Universe as I transform." Breathe a little deeper now and begin to envision yourself flying as a bat with great agility and stability as you rise above the fears and challenges associated with this change. If you see obstacles coming your way, nimbly dart to avoid them. Continue with your flight until you feel strong and confident. Then, visualize a cave where you'll be safe, and swoop down toward it, latching your feet to the wall and hanging upside down. From this visualized position, breathe into your heart center. Emerge from the cave with the strength and clarity that bat provided.

"Bat medicine supported me through one of my life. During this time, the bat revealed itself had deeply moving and reverent encounters eye with the largest bat I've ever witnessed. being on such an honest, vulnerable level that it lably wept. For the following four months, holding some monumental fears that would need to be life I was ready for. It was through bat's energetic shift low vibrations to high vibrations. By tuning bat cave and fully embody my truth and power. friend and guide."

the most powerful shamanic passageways of
as my power animal, and shortly thereafter, I
with live bats in Bali—including seeing eye-to-
During this experience, I felt connected to this
blasted open my heart and soul and I uncontrol-
the potent love of bat, I came face-to-face with
transcended in order for me to get to the level of
medicine that I was able to turn fear to love and
in to bat energy, I was able to rise out of the dark
I am forever grateful for this powerfully loving

—Alyson Charles

BEAR

GROUNDED POWER • STABILIZING COMFORT • CONSCIOUSNESS • SURRENDER INTO DIVINE SUPPORT • COURAGE

WHEN TO WORK WITH ME:

When you need to be energetically recharged, when you need comfort, when you want to feel held by the love of the universe, when you want to learn to go within and trust yourself, when you want to feel more grounded, when you need to stand in your power

ENERGY MEDICINE:

If you are experiencing a time of awakening, a time where previously held illusions or denials are now releasing and coming to light, tap into my support as you rise and change.

Honor the rhythms of your life and recognize whether now is the time for you to rest and cultivate new ideas and new foundations or whether now is the time for you to step out of your cave and present yourself to the world. Remember, you cannot hide forever.

I am a powerful reminder for you to get more grounded. Walk barefoot on the Earth, give her great thanks, and allow yourself to receive the Earth medicine to stabilize and root your power.

You are at a place in life when you are ready to unearth the incredible ancient wisdom, intuition, and inner power that has previously lain dormant. It is time for you to bring forward new abilities.

Do not seek outwardly for answers right now. Trust yourself. Do practices that take you within. Listen to the guidance that is revealed from inside of you and heed it.

Remember that by having the courage to realize who you truly are and by authentically being in and of the world, you can truly be fulfilled.

Great Spirit lives through me and this infinite support is here for you now.

Are you making decisions from a place of inner power? If you go within, you will find your way home.

POWER PRACTICE:

Find a place to sit or lie comfortably. Close your eyes and envision yourself sitting on the earth with a huge bear sitting directly behind you. Envision yourself leaning back completely into this bear, your back against its chest, and let your entire being (physically, spiritually, emotionally, mentally, energetically) be held by it. Not one drop of yourself is clinging or trying to hold yourself up; you are totally releasing into the bear.

From this position, tell the bear you are ready to accept its support and receive the messages, medicines, and guidance it wishes to provide for your highest, greatest good. Continue being held by the bear until you feel energetically recharged. Thank the bear for being there for you, and gently open your eyes. In the days ahead, be aware of how your intuition is guiding you and be sure to heed it. This is bear's energy awakening the inner wisdom within you.

PROTECTION, COURAGE, AND STRENGTH

In the ancient Chinese practice of feng shui—the art of bringing balance and harmony to a space—placing a representation of a bear at the main entrance of the home is said to bring protection to the space. Bears also symbolize masculine energies in the world and their gallbladders are said to have strong yang properties—properties that invoke courage and strength.

BEAVER

NIGHTTIME • BUILDER • AT HOME • TEETH • TEAMWORK • DREAMS • CLOSE FAMILY • OPEN-MINDEDNESS

WHEN TO WORK WITH ME:

When you want to build something strong, when you want healthy relationships and team dynamics, when you want to go after your dreams, when you want a happy home, when you want to balance work and play, when you want to get out of your own way

ENERGY MEDICINE:

I carry with me some of the most powerful energies of creation and construction. Have you started and stopped a project? I'm your reminder to see it all the way through. Remember, a strong foundation is important, and steady and thorough are better than rushed and done.

Remain pliable during the creative processes. Be open to ways that can actually strengthen your end result.

While I possess the ability to work long and hard, I also remind you to take needed self-care breaks to recharge your batteries.

Check in with yourself to assess whether you are self-sabotaging at this time. Are you blocking or "damming up" your own success due to unconscious fears?

I remind you that with strong family connections and proper teamwork, powerful visions cannot only become reality, but also exceed far beyond your greatest imagination.

Is there a dream you gave up on that still stirs in your soul? Swim in meditative waters to inquire within whether you should activate that dream again.

POWER PRACTICE:

Beavers use their large, orange, iron-coated (the iron gives them extra strength) front teeth to make their way through wood. They work steadily and patiently to finish their mind-blowing building projects that serve our planet. In this practice, we'll call on beaver to help us chew things over in our mind until the answers reveal themselves. Find a quiet place to sit with your journal, and write the following questions down on the page:

- What have I been procrastinating on and what fear has driven that procrastination?
- Is there a conversation that I need to have that I've been putting off?
- What big dream am I not following through on?

Now, tune in to the image of beaver working through a large log as you answer each question, writing down the first thoughts that come to mind without hesitation.

When you're finished, read over what you've written. Now it's up to you—with beaver by your side—to take matters into your own hands and do something about the answers that presented themselves. Call upon beaver medicine to amplify your ability to get up, get going, and see things through.

LODGES AND DAMS

Beavers make their homes in dome-shaped structures called lodges, which they build using grass, sticks, and moss, plastered with mud. Beavers create dams to surround their lodges with water, offering them some protection from predators. Beaver dams can increase biodiversity, filter water, and restore delicate ecosystems. Some modern ecologists call beavers the "Earth's kidneys" because of the vital role they play in freshwater ecosystems.

BEE

FERTILITY • ROYALTY • HARMONY • COMMUNITY • CREATIVE INSPIRATION

WHEN TO WORK WITH ME:

When you're ready to achieve the "impossible," when you want to tap into your royal roots, when you want to deeply connect with true community and family, when you're ready to "pollinate" special projects and relationships

ENERGY MEDICINE:

I represent harmonious community. If you want to find like-minded humans who will align to support you or help a group reach a goal, call upon me.

I am royalty and know how to honor my divine power. Work with me to further empower these traits in you.

I am a reminder for you that it is very possible to balance productivity with making space for sacred, mindful moments. Think of all that my fellow bees and I create: honey, pollen, propolis. I am central to the gloriousness of life and all the nature and abundance that surrounds us.

Celebrate. Have you forgotten that there is so much to cherish and be grateful for? Failing to see all the treasures within yourself and in your life can create bitterness and low-vibration energy. See your earthly experience with fresh eyes and heart.

Call upon my pollinating energy for fertility, sex, and love. Or look to me as a symbol of a fertile time in your life, a time to birth new ideas, projects, or children.

Aerodynamically, my body is not built to fly and, scientifically speaking, I shouldn't be able to. Yet I fly with skill and confidence. I carry with me the magic that *nothing* is impossible. Widen your visions and expand, expand, expand.

POWER PRACTICE:

In this practice, you will manifest the royal bee energy inside of you. Find a quiet place to sit comfortably, then close your eyes and visualize yourself sitting on top of a very large honeycomb that is filled with bees making honey. Relax your body and thank the bees for being on your support team and for making their rich honey, bowing your head in reverence and gratitude to them. Then begin to imagine your *grandest* visions for your life. Expand your visions like never before—the things you want to accomplish, the places you want to go—don't hold anything back. Now visualize yourself reaching down into the honeycomb and pulling up a handful of honey. Begin to rub your hands over your body, imagining that you're covering yourself with the bees' honey. This honey is an activator of your visions; it will bless and purify you with the bees' medicine. The sticky, sweet substance will attract whatever you need to manifest your visions and allow those things to *stick* to you. Once you have finished covering yourself in honey, sit up proudly on the honeycomb as the royal bee you are, feeling strong and grounded, and give thanks once more for the bees that have provided you with their support and honey. Then, open your eyes, welcoming your bright future and carrying the feeling of being basked in honey through the days ahead.

AN ANCIENT SYMBOL

Bees have been revered and worshipped in many cultures around the globe. The earliest records of beekeeping appear in the Cuavas de la Araña, caves in Spain that feature ancient paintings, including an image of a person harvesting honey. Though it's difficult to date, some estimate that the painting could be as much as 8,000 years old.

The San peoples of the Kalahari Desert tell a story of a bee that carried a praying mantis across a river. Exhausted from its efforts, the bee managed to plant a seed inside the mantis before dying. That seed eventually grew to be the first human on Earth.

The bee also appears throughout ancient Greek culture: the Greek god Aristaeus, son of Zeus, was known as the god of beekeeping and honey, and the image of a bee was associated with Potnia, a goddess of nature worshipped by some Myceneans and known as "Pure Mother Bee."

"I was taught that the honeybee's medicine and message is of a very high caliber, not to be treated lightly or ignored. When she comes calling, she is taking time away from her day to bring assistance, guidance, assurance, or inspiration. When I received a visit from the honeybee, I was arrogant in my resistance to her advice. Walking home, the spring grass tender and moist under my bare feet, I was completely at ease, relaxed, and without any concerns. I wanted to feel the cold, wet grass under a tree that I saw next to a wall, so I gleefully pranced over to the shady area and buried my feet in the clover-covered grass. I forgot all my manners and ground my feet into the wetness of the clover, delighted by the coolness, without a please or thank you.

"Suddenly, I felt the hot, painful pinch of a honeybee sting, like a glass shard on the sole of my foot. My husband pulled the stinger out. I cooled the throbbing pain in the grass's dampness. By the next morning, my sole was swollen purple and as hot as if it had a fever, but there was no pain or discomfort—only a constant itching from the inflammation. I was angry that she had personally visited in order to make sure the message was not only accepted but also implemented. The message? I was to go from a cloistered life back to the public, to the people. Finally, I relented. I cried, I was sad, I was angry, I was ready . . . Life will *live itself, as us, through us*. The World has come knocking, and She is here."

—Tatyana Rae

HEALER AND MENTOR

BEETLE

OPTIMISM • POWER OF THE SUN • RESURRECTION • CHANGE • THE DESERT • REEMERGENCE • ENLIGHTENMENT

WHEN TO WORK WITH ME:

When you want to be more optimistic, when you're going through major change or rebirth, when you are ready for spiritual advancement, when you're ready to embody your full power, when you're ready to bring forward new life, when you want more ease, when you want to get through hard times with grace

ENERGY MEDICINE:

Could you improve your ability to have more optimistic thoughts? Investigate whether an addiction to worry may be at play and, if so, remind yourself to keep your thoughts pointed toward the sun.

When you are ready to navigate through all of life (even the deepest hardships) with grace and ease, call upon me to support you.

If you've been experiencing intense spiritual awakenings and realizations, and if you're willing to see the lessons and grow, then trust that these fires of transformation are ascending you.

Don't fight the changes that are revealing for you. At first, they may feel like foreign territory, but remember that the thing you're resisting could be the precise ingredient for you to embody your whole power.

I bring forth expanded energies of spiritual ascension and enlightenment. Are you heeding your soul's call to live a more spiritual life?

Infinity can sometimes best be understood by heading up to the cosmos and feeling or seeing the infinite space and infinite possibilities. I empower you to remember these ancient truths now.

POWER PRACTICE:

In this practice, you'll journey inward to find the silver linings and lessons in difficult experiences. Get out a journal and a pen and call upon beetle to join you in this practice. The scarab beetle is known for its magnificent ability to extract treasure during challenging times. Close your eyes and see yourself as a beetle traversing the desert, moving across dunes through heat and sandstorms, always walking toward the sun. After you spend a few moments in this experience, open your eyes. Now, turn to your journal, and begin to write about an experience that first appeared terribly hard, bad, or unfair, but eventually turned out to be a blessing in disguise. Perhaps it was a breakup, a situation at work, or a period of change. Continue to write your stream of consciousness, exploring how the challenge ended up providing great miracles and richness in your life. Reflect on this experience and the unending spiritual support you have at all times, knowing more deeply that even the most difficult experiences are serving your highest, greatest, earthly good. As you close the journal, thank beetle for working with you and invite it to continue to guide you to living your most spiritually aligned life.

SACRED SCARAB BEETLE

Ancient Egyptians revered the scarab beetle so deeply that during burials, they would often place an amulet of a scarab beetle on the deceased person's heart to protect them in the afterlife. For the living, the amulet would shield against illness or negative energy. The scarab beetle is a symbol of the ancient Egyptian god Khepri and also the sun god Ra, when he was in the form of Khepri, and often signifies resurrection and optimism for a greater life.

"The scarab beetle showed me many years ago grounded force and energies of Earth. My ethers, swimming with the cosmos, being more in the Egyptian section of a store deciding on 'feeling into' each of them energetically, a scarab like it was dropping not just my hand but also into the bin with a swiftness, 'That's definitely my eyes, and said, 'Or maybe that's the exact nearly fell to the ground when I held that beetle Maybe you need that grounded energy.' My truth, and I had an instantaneous realization this planet's energy field. From that moment Great Mother Earth's medicines and teachings, of both Earth and Sky, one of the biggest game that I had been unconsciously resisting the unconscious comfort zone was being up in the out of my body than in it. One fateful day, I was which talisman to purchase. As I was holding and talisman that had a very grounded energy felt pulling my entire being to the floor. I tossed it back not the one.' My colleague paused, looked me in one you need.' I reminded him that my body in my palm, to which he replied, 'Precisely. entire being resonated with what he said as full about my unconscious resistance to being in forward, I dedicated practices to getting to know which led me to being in balanced embodiment changers on my spiritual journey."

—Alyson Charles

BLACK JAGUAR

THE MOON • GUARDIAN • RECLAMATION OF POWER • CLAIRAUDIENT • DECISIVENESS • GALACTIC

WHEN TO WORK WITH ME:

When you're going through uncertainty and change, when you're ready to do shadow work, when working with the moon, when you're ready for a complete rebirth, when you're ready to reclaim your power

ENERGY MEDICINE:

I work with your shadow, which is key to you embodying your full power. What aspects of yourself that you've previously deemed shameful or "bad" are you now ready to face and healthily integrate?

I represent the ability to be comfortable, capable, and strong in solitude. This is key for becoming sovereign.

I help you get in sync with and work with lunar (moon) energies that will bring you strength.

I bring you energies of being highly capable and talented in a multitude of ways and the ability to focus on what you want and going for it.

I can activate feminine prowess within you—does your mother, goddess, or high priestess within want to emerge? Call on me to help you integrate those energies.

I am a reminder that facing darkness and death are not to be feared, as they allow for your mystic wisdom, deeper trust, and rebirth to occur.

I will empower your courage and enlightenment, along with your ability to be your authentic self. I am your guide in your journey of reclaiming your power.

With me, I help you embrace the unknown, the darkness of the void, the phases in your life when you are thrust into spaces with much uncertainty. While fears may rise up, work with me to remind yourself that this is also the space of infinite possibilities and miracles. You can emerge greater than ever before.

POWER PRACTICE:

In this practice, you'll work with black jaguar (also called black panther) to come into your personal power. During the new moon, sit in meditation and call upon sacred panther to be with you as you meditate. Envision its powerful, sleek body moving in slow circles around you. Take energizing and clearing inhalations and relaxing exhalations until you feel present and centered. Ask black jaguar to come forth in your meditation and share ideas on how you can connect more with your true power by asking, "Black jaguar, what can I do to grow my power?" Ask as many times as necessary and make note of any messages and feelings that arise in response. Before completing the meditation, ask that black jaguar remain with you to empower these changes in your life.

"On my first shamanic drum journey to meet a power animal, black jaguar showed up. She was magnificent, graceful, dark as night, powerful, and loving.

"After that first encounter, I often had lucid dreams where I was with black jaguar, running or just sitting with her, with my head on her body. Looking back, I now know that those moments were a period of deepening the connection and teaching me to trust her.

"A few years later, I had advanced in my shamanic studies and it was time to go on a vision quest—three days alone with no food, only water, a few sacred objects, and a whistle to use in case of an emergency. I anticipated my quest with a lot of trepidation. I was a city girl from Cameroon. I had never been in nature alone, never been camping, and never pitched a tent.

"Once I set up my campsite, I took in my surroundings. I was all alone. Night was coming fast. There were sounds around me, sounds I had never heard before and could not identify. That's when real fear set in. I sat in front of my tent, listening to every sound.

"When my fear became overwhelming, I started meditating and praying, and that's when something extraordinary happened: I had a vivid vision. Black jaguar came to let me know without words that she would be there, protecting and guiding me. That reassurance allowed me to spend those three days in trust and without fear.

"I realized that black jaguar had truly become an ally. I started consciously calling on black jaguar to work with me, to guide me and help me heal. Since then, I have been working with her for myself and have integrated more and more of her qualities. Black jaguar represents the silence of the night, the frequency of black, the unknown, the shadow. It symbolizes the power of silence, like when a black jaguar quietly hunts or stalks its prey. It shows me that it is important to discern when to make your presence known and when to stay hidden.

"Black jaguar also represents acute sensitivity to vibrations, the importance of paying attention to your emotions, and hearing the words that are unsaid and the feelings that need to be conveyed. It helps showcase the hidden gifts you should be sharing with the world, including your beauty, power, strength, grace, and knowledge. She understands chaos and how to move with courage through the dark times of life. There's a great mysticism within the black jaguar's unblinking stare. It seems like it can look right through you and see your innermost thoughts and feelings and your deepest secrets. Black jaguar teaches you to trust in your personal instincts and innate wisdom."

—Dr. Marie Mbouni

MD, SHAMAN

SACRED PRAYER • EARTH AND SPIRIT UNITY • DIRECTION • ABUNDANCE • ENDURANCE • GRATITUDE • HONOR • SERVICE

WHEN TO WORK WITH ME:

When you need to reconnect with gratitude and abundance, when you're feeling strong and want to support others in need, when you want to be sure you're on the best track, when you want to manifest your highest good

ENERGY MEDICINE:

My medicine is full of gratitude and abundance. Have you been busying yourself with trivial things and forgetting to express reverence for all you have? I remind you to zoom out and take stock of your blessings.

Are you ready for more? Look around at all the gifts you have in your life. Then work with me to open your energetic gateways and invite even more abundance into your life and your experience.

Float up to a higher perspective, where you can see the miracles of it all. Then, come back down to Earth embodying that reverent perspective with power and stability. Move from there.

I bring miracles, prosperity, and blessings. This is more than possibility; this is reality.

I remind you to use your power and abilities to lift up those currently in need. If you're feeling strong and centered, who could use some of that uplifting support? Which charities for endangered animals can you donate to?

I share the ancient truth that to manifest all that will positively serve you, you must work in conjunction with Source. Allow for it to organically unfold, and honor and respect Great Mother Earth.

POWER PRACTICE:

This practice taps into buffalo's sense of direction and its powerful stampedes—a formidable, collective run as a herd. Next time you want clarity on a decision, close your eyes and see yourself standing in a field. Out in the field are two circles: Within circle one is the word describing the first possible path to take or decision to make. Within circle two is the word describing the other option or path. Next, call upon sacred buffalo to come in and support you. Imagine that a massive herd of more than a hundred buffalo enter the field. Ask them to stampede with full power, divinity, and strength to the circle that holds the choice that will serve your highest, greatest, earthly good and the greatest good of all. Watch and allow the buffalo to stampede to the circle, showing you the way.

MOVING WITH THE MAJORITY

African buffalo herds choose which direction to move in by consensus. Each buffalo points its head in the direction it wants to travel, and then they all move in the direction the majority voted for, led by the head female in the herd.

HONORING THE BUFFALO

The Native North American Plains tribes perform a buffalo dance to embody and honor this sacred animal. They pay respect to the animal's strength and unity, wear the skins of the buffalo, and have an annual Buffalo Dance festival at the same time that the herds come back to their land.

BULL

FERTILITY • COMING TOGETHER • STUBBORNNESS • STAMINA • ACTIVATING FEMININITY • INCREDIBLE STRENGTH • CONFIDENCE

WHEN TO WORK WITH ME:

When you need immense strength, when you want to be a better leader, when you want to have a baby, when you want more abundance, when you want balanced masculine and feminine energies, when you don't want to be stubborn or operate from ego, when you want steadfast belief in working toward a goal

ENERGY MEDICINE:

Are you feeling a bit too "fiery" inside? Is aggravation or stubbornness taking hold? Call upon me to connect you with lunar energies and bring about more calm.

I'm here to remind you that you can be a strong leader without being a tyrant. There is incredible power that comes from leading with your feminine strengths. Kindness and astute leadership do go hand in hand.

I embody strength to move what may seem like insurmountable obstacles. It's time for you to take charge and give things all you've got.

Having both divine feminine and divine masculine energies activated is key to thriving. I assist in awakening and balancing these aspects within you.

Are you willing to delegate? Can you trust enough to have someone else tend to the tasks that you know are draining you? I urge you to lead through deciding to have help. You can begin by asking me to help you in doing this.

Fertility is one of my biggest medicines. Call upon me to awaken your abilities to receive new creative energies and give birth to new life.

POWER PRACTICE:

In this practice, we'll work on softening challenging energy. Bull is often associated with negative, difficult traits: "bull-headed," "stubborn as a bull," "a raging bull." Close your eyes and envision a bull displaying incredibly frustrated energy—stamping its feet, pacing irritably, steam coming out its nostrils. Hold the bull's gaze and look deeper into its eyes. Speak softly to it; let it know that despite its reputation, you can see the truth of kindness and love, the calm at the center of its soul. Watch as the bull's eyes soften. Now, holding this image in your mind, think of a situation in your life that's been clouded with frustration or irritability. Consider how you can open yourself up to a softer energy. If you were to let yourself be guided by this gentler, more open place, how could your situation improve? Meditate on these possibilities. Before you open your eyes, thank the bull for showing you the way.

THE BULL THROUGHOUT HISTORY

The sacred bull appears in cultures throughout history. In the Hindu faith, the deity Nandi is worshipped as the sacred bull calf, the gatekeeper and vehicle for the Hindu god Shiva. The ancient Celtics revered the bull for its physical strength, strong will, and virility. Some Celts kept a symbol of the bull near their bed to increase sexual strength and endurance.

The bull also held significance in Ancient Egypt. Bulls, which were used frequently for plowing farms along the Nile, symbolized fertility and agriculture. Egyptians worshipped the deity Apis, a sacred bull and the son of Hathor, an important goddess in Egyptian religion. Mummified bulls have been recovered from ancient Egyptian burial sites, indicating their cultural importance.

BUTTERFLY

METAMORPHOSIS • JOYOUS FLIGHT • LIGHTHEARTEDNESS • SHAPE-SHIFTING • SYNCHRONICITY • BEAUTY

WHEN TO WORK WITH ME:

When you're ready to evolve with joy, when you want to be filled with lightheartedness, when you're ready to get in sync with the energy of the Universe, when you're ready to accept that the magic of life is right here, right now

ENERGY MEDICINE:

I am your reminder to not take life too seriously. If the energies around or within you have felt harsh, heavy, or dense, give yourself permission to lighten your vibe and be free.

The color, magic, and aliveness of this earthly life is all here, just waiting for you to be able to see. Through doing soul-level work, you'll access this lens more.

Do you believe that great transformation can be done with joy and ease? If yes, you're correct, and I'm here to amplify the sweet nectar in your life. Examine my flight patterns, and observe my effortless ability to dance with the joy and sweetness of this life.

While all change is truly positive, it's important to know which phase of change you're in. Are you in the cocooning phase, where it's important to rest and germinate? In the birthing phase, where the new you is just ready to emerge? Or the full flight stage, where the change is now embodied?

Remember that by staying connected to Great Spirit and Great Mother Earth, you will be best aligned in achieving your goals with divinity and grace.

POWER PRACTICE:

This practice will help you cultivate joy and lightheartedness by working with butterfly's flight. Close your eyes and imagine you're watching a beautiful butterfly fluttering in a lush garden, moving with ease and lightness from flower to flower. What activity can you visualize yourself stepping into that will allow you to feel this sense of joy and playfulness? It could be dancing, singing, collecting flowers, swimming in the ocean, rolling around in the grass. Whatever you choose, commit to staying present in this visualization experience. Let go of past and future thoughts as you embody the butterfly's lightness and liberation. When you've finished, close your eyes and thank butterfly for bringing this reminder into your life and ask it to help you keep things light in the future.

A SYMBOL OF TRANSFORMATION

In Irish folklore, the butterfly is a symbol of transformation and creation, a being that can cross between realms. In Greek mythology, the butterfly was considered a symbol of the soul and regeneration. Greek philosophers compared the evolution of a caterpillar into a butterfly to the transformation of man from an ignorant creature to a noble and transcendent being, capable of ascending into the higher atmosphere of light and truth. The soul was contained in the body as in a chrysalis and in time it would liberate itself and become a creature of exquisite beauty.

CAMEL

RESOURCEFULNESS • COMMITMENT • FAITH • ADAPTABILITY • DESERT MAGIC • INNER POWER • GLOBAL MINDEDNESS

WHEN TO WORK WITH ME:

When you are going through a tough time, when you feel like giving up, when you need to be reminded of your strength, when you need power to continue, when you're in harsh environments or situations, when you feel alone

ENERGY MEDICINE:

I am here to give you a loving kick in the butt and remind you that you can get through any challenge. But first you must break out of a victim mentality. Muster up your strength and tune in to the gift of your self-sufficiency. You have everything it takes to get through this.

If you are feeling beaten down by life and exhausted, remember that there is always a deeper power source within you to be found. Keep going. You can do it.

I bring wonders of this world and Universe to you—are you ready to expand your conscious awareness to one that embraces miracles? If yes, I am your guide.

If you have a project, vision, or goal that is long term, I am your greatest ally in bringing it all to fruition with steadiness, productive pace, calm, and confidence.

Is your environment unhealthy or harsh lately? Work with my medicine to cultivate a fierce commitment and to hold the line to make it through with faith. A positive mindset is your key right now. I represent the connection point to treasures, new and better places, culture, and expansion.

POWER PRACTICE:

In this practice, you will tune in to camel's profound ability to continue putting one foot in front of the other, no matter how long the journey or how challenging the conditions. For the next week, at least, make a commitment to call upon camel to be with you as you wake up early each morning and watch the sunrise. As you gaze toward the sun, allow the medicine of the solar energy to activate you. Infuse into that inner strength and fire so you can go about your day feeling empowered, fueled, and committed to finding your way forward.

BUILT TO ENDURE

The camel's strength, endurance, and adaptability are demonstrated in its physiology. The camel's hump, which is made of fat, can act as a source of energy when there's no access to food. The camel has a tough lining within its mouth, which allows it to eat cactus if that's the only available source of food. Camels can also cool their brains in extreme heat to protect themselves.

CREATED FROM CLAY

There is an ancient Hindu myth in which the first camel is created by Lord Shiva, an important Hindu deity. In this story, Shiva's lover, Parvati, shaped a five-legged animal out of clay and asked Shiva to make it come alive. Shiva initially declined, fearing the animal would have a tough life, but eventually he decided to fold the fifth leg over the animal's back, creating the camel's signature hump, and brought the clay creation to life.

CATERPILLAR

INFINITE POTENTIAL • RESURRECTION • DIVINE TIMING • NEW IDEAS • RELEASING THE OLD • DEVELOPMENT

WHEN TO WORK WITH ME:

When you need to remember you're exactly where you're meant to be, when you need new inspiration and ideas, when you need clarity before making a decision, when you're ready for the next phase of life

ENERGY MEDICINE:

Before you jump into any big action or decisions, take a breath and ask whether a strong foundation has been set yet.

I am here to have you do an honest, inner inquiry—what are you ready to let go of so you can allow your life to open to new possibilities?

Now is a perfect time to meditate on the following: "What new ideas are ready to make their way to me? I am open to receiving new inspiration now."

I am here to remind you that no one should seek to gain strength by tearing another down. Protect your emotional health. Stand up for your right to be treated respectfully.

Trust in divine timing. While your ego may want things to look a certain way or happen at a certain pace, when you truly trust that you're exactly where you're meant to be, stress and pressure dissolve away.

POWER PRACTICE:

Get a piece of paper and a pen. On the far right of your page, draw a circle and within it write a goal you have. Then close your eyes and meditate on the image of a caterpillar slowly inching along and call upon its medicine to create a strong foundation with magical properties. Open your eyes and ask yourself, "What steps do I need to take to ensure this goal manifests with the best support possible?" Now draw five lines that lead to your circle and along each line write one thing you need to do to create a strong foundation for that goal to materialize. Ask caterpillar to be with you in the process of taking each step. Place this piece of paper on your altar or somewhere you can see it each day, and hold yourself accountable to move toward your vision in this intentional way.

"For Australian Aboriginal people, Dreaming represents the time when the Ancestral Spirits progressed over the land, creating life and important geographic formations and sites.

"Back in Dreamtime, there were three giant caterpillars, as big as the mountains we see today, in the desert in what is now called the Australian outback, looking for food.

"An emu, the largest native bird in Australia, came along and thought the caterpillars would be a good meal, so it bent down and picked a piece off one of the caterpillars. The caterpillars went into defensive mode, bringing up their stingers around their bodies. The emu ran away so it wouldn't get stung. That's why the emu is so fast today: because it had to run away from the caterpillars.

"After the emu left, the caterpillars turned to stone. They couldn't move—they didn't want to. The injured caterpillar and its missing piece represented a part of their tribe, and since a piece of it was missing, the caterpillars wanted to stay in the spot the injury had happened and remain connected. This is symbolic of a loyal community. Caterpillars are frequently painted in Aboriginal art today because they signify a tribe. They also symbolize growth and the importance of taking in all the nutrients and spiritual lessons needed to turn into a colorful butterfly.

"The Dreamtime caterpillars can still be seen today as the mountains known as the MacDonnell Ranges, bordering Alice Springs in Australia's Northern Territory. If you visit one day, and I hope you do, you will see a large gap in this range. That gap is the caterpillar's missing piece that the emu ate.

"It might sound strange that caterpillars were once as large as mountains, but there is still a great deal to learn about Australia's ancient megaflora and megafauna, these animals that collectively died out in a mass extinction about forty-six thousand years ago. The Dreaming is still vitally important to today's Aboriginal people. It gives us a social and spiritual base and links us to our cultural heritage."

—Jasper Ntjalka Williams

THE HUMAN CATERPILLAR,
AUSTRALIAN ABORIGINAL

PACING • SHAPE-SHIFTING • PERCEPTION • ENVIRONMENT • MYSTERY • DIVINE FLOW • METHOD • THIRD EYE (PSYCHIC INSIGHT)

WHEN TO WORK WITH ME:

When you need your energy to be balanced, when you want to embrace change, when you want to embody your full power, when you want to open your supernatural abilities, when you want stronger intuition, when you want to see truth, when you want a better game plan

ENERGY MEDICINE:

I am here to remind you to be aware of the opportunities all around you. Ask yourself how you can more actively move toward your goal.

I remind you of the importance of seeing truth and listening to your intuition. Blinding yourself to the intentions of others won't serve you.

I represent the power of surrender and flow. If you have been pushing too hard, work with me to learn how to trust and let go.

If your environment is changing, remember that you have the full power to harmoniously align with the new. Work with the energies of the new space, and shift in the ways you are guided to.

I remind you to face all aspects of yourself (shadow and light), as this lets you shine fully, be at peace, and truly thrive.

POWER PRACTICE:

Some chameleons can change colors, and in this practice, you'll work with color healing to reveal what practices can support you in this moment. Be sure to go through this exercise step by step, without skipping ahead to the list of colors.

Begin by closing your eyes and connecting with your breath. Imagine yourself with chameleon skin that can change to any color of the rainbow.

When you feel centered and calm, ask yourself, "If I could be any color of the rainbow today, what would I be?"

When you have your answer, open your eyes and find the properties of the color you selected below:

- Red: It's time for grounding and body connection. Make time for reconnecting to your body through massage, physical activity, or breathwork.
- Orange: You have creative energies that want to express themselves. Make time to be artistic, write, or collaborate on something new.
- Yellow: Are you holding back your full joy and authentic expression? It's time to share your truth with the world.
- Green: Your heart has so much love to give. Who can you call, what charity can you support, where can you volunteer, or in what ways can you be gentler and more compassionate with yourself?
- Blue: Now is the time to be vocal. Sing, chant, or have the conversation you've been putting off.
- Purple: Divine support is all around you. Now is the time to open up your spiritual pathways to connect to unseen realms.

KEEN PERCEPTION

In addition to being able to change color, a chameleon can also move its eyes independently of each other, which allows it to get a sweeping view of any situation, making them a perfect representation for perception and seeing truth.

CHICKEN

DIVINATION • SACRIFICE • DEPTH • SACRED PAUSE • ENTHUSIASM • DANCE • SOCIABILITY • INSIGHT

WHEN TO WORK WITH ME:

When you want to speak with confidence, when you want to step out into the world bravely, when you want to move your body freely, when you want to see through people's intentions and energies, when you want to expand into a life of service

ENERGY MEDICINE:

I bring forward potent medicine so that you can be of service for the highest, greatest good of all. By devoting to this way of life, you are sure to experience miracles beyond imagination.

Remember, your words have great power. Before writing or speaking, tune in to the intention and desired energetic imprint you have for your expressions.

Check in with yourself. Is your head running the show lately? It's time to take a pause, connect with the deeper, heart-centered part of yourself, and move from there.

I represent bold energies and great social abilities. Call upon me to get you out of hiding and into the world with courage and ease.

I am known for my dancing power. When was the last time you let yourself be free in your movements? Remember the magic of moving your body without a care in the world.

Because of my prophetic abilities, you can call upon me to look over you and your family and to strengthen your discernment for who and what amplifies or negates your experience.

POWER PRACTICE:

Dance is one of chicken's most powerful medicinal attributes. To activate and amplify the powers of chicken, this practice will help you get into your body and embrace freedom through dance. Set aside at least 20 minutes, take off your shoes and socks, put on a high-vibe song that activates your spirit, and let your body move freely, envisioning chickens scratching and pecking at the ground. If you can, dance barefoot outside—connecting with Great Mother Earth will enhance the benefits of this practice.

THE PRARIE CHICKEN DANCE

The Prairie Chicken Dance is a traditional Native American Blackfeet dance that honors the chicken's courtship display during the spring. This dance is said to have come about after a young Blackfeet man killed a prairie chicken and was visited later by the spirit of that chicken. The chicken asked the man why he killed him, and the man explained that he needed to feed his family. The man and the chicken spirit then agreed to a deal: The man would learn the chicken dance and teach all of his people, or his life would be taken.

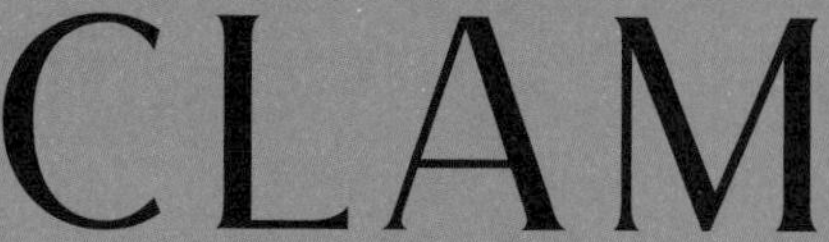

HAPPINESS • EARTH NOURISHMENT • INWARD WORK •
FREEDOM • HIDDEN TALENTS • DESIRE TO "STEP OUT"

WHEN TO WORK WITH ME:

When you're ready to stop hiding your talents and gifts, when you want to invite more happiness, when you're ready to put in the inner work to experience true freedom, when you're ready to transcend fears that have held you back, when you're ready to take responsibility for your life

ENERGY MEDICINE:

I represent happiness and freedom. If you have found yourself in a period of feeling down, take honest inventory of what fear-based narratives are keeping you playing small.

Have you been holding yourself back? Are you aware of talents inside you that you've allowed to stay hidden? This is your wake-up call to give your gifts room to express themselves.

Keep doing the inner work. The hidden gems and treasures are typically found just beyond where we think our threshold lies. Going a touch deeper may give you the miracle you seek.

If greater inner peace is what you seek, ask yourself how you can live in better harmony with nature and your own family and home.

To suppress your true light and authentic self out of fear of rejection or judgment gives your power away to others. Trust that with your gifts you were also given the tools to fully live them.

I remind you that taking full responsibility for the quality of your experiences, internal state, and life is key. Are you blaming someone else for any discomfort?

POWER PRACTICE:

Have you ever heard the saying "happy as a clam"? That statement is likely derived from "as happy as a clam at high tide." During high tide, clams are protected by water, making them hard for fishermen to dig up.

In this meditation practice, you will connect with true happiness. Begin by finding a quiet place to sit with your eyes closed. Envision yourself as a closed clam hiding at low tide—tight, stuffed, suppressed, and stifled. Spend a moment in this feeling. Then begin to explore the inside of your shell, and imagine discovering a beautiful pearl. Examine the shining pearl, taking in its colors and energies. Ask the pearl, "What can I do that will allow more happiness into my heart and life?" Ask the pearl this question as many times as necessary until the answer is revealed. Once you have your answer, envision your clamshell being gently enveloped by the high tide. Feel the water above you as your chest and heart center expand; feel the liberation, expansion, breath, and freedom within you. Say the words, "I become at one with the pearls of my happiness now." In the weeks to come, follow the wisdom this meditation brought forth.

FROM IRRITATION TO CREATION

The pearls found inside clams can take years to form. They begin to develop when an irritant, like a shell fragment or parasite, gets stuck inside the clam. The clam's natural defenses begin to coat the irritant with a fluid. This continued coating of the irritant forms a pearl. Depending on the type and location of the clam, it can take anywhere from 6 months to more than 3 years for the pearl to reach maturity.

CONDOR

SPIRITUAL ADVANCEMENT • HEART INTELLIGENCE • FREE FLIGHT • FEMININE POWER • WIND AND AIR • CONSCIOUS AWARENESS

WHEN TO WORK WITH ME:

When you are ready to see truth, when you are ready to awaken spiritually, when you are ready to activate your feminine power, when you are ready to expand beyond confines, when you're ready to transcend limiting patterns and fears, when you're ready for more freedom

ENERGY MEDICINE:

I signal that messages from the unseen realms are here for you. Be aware of what your ancestors, spirit guides, intuitive knowing, and Great Spirit may be trying to communicate to you.

If you are feeling called to the spiritual path, call upon me to protect and guide you with ease.

Balance is important for you right now; take an honest look where you can improve with this.

Have you been connecting with Great Spirit and the powers of the wind and air daily? I remind you that in order to have your earthly life in order, your connection to Spirit is essential.

How can you show up more aligned with your authentic truth and communication? Ask yourself whether you are truly sharing what needs to be said and expressed to others from your heart.

Are you ready to finally take the leap that your soul has been urging you to? I'm here to empower you in this next, needed step. Trust what your spiritual inner knowing is telling you.

POWER PRACTICE:

In this meditation journey you'll work with chakras and condor energy to open up the channel between yourself here on Earth and Great Spirit—the cosmos, universe, and unseen realms. You can do this alone, reading and doing each part step by step, you can ask a partner to slowly read the steps as you follow along, or you can be guided through a version of this practice on my website (alysoncharles.com).

Find a quiet place to sit comfortably. Close your eyes and connect with your body and breath. Tune in to the base of your spine or tailbone area (this is where the first, red, root chakra lives). Allow your breath and the power of condor to cleanse, clear, and invigorate this space.

Now envision a cord beginning to grow from your tailbone, grounding down into Great Mother Earth. Call for condor to join you, to become one with you, as the two of you follow your cord to see where it takes you within the layers of Earth. Take your grounding cord and condor into the place where you want to anchor into Earth. Perhaps it's the hard rocky layers, or maybe it's the alive, molten metal inner core. Anchor your cord. Ask that the messages, medicine, and guidance that will serve your highest, greatest, earthly good and the highest good of all be sent to you via condor rising it up your cord now. Be aware. Feel. See. Hear.

Now move with condor to the center of your chest where your heart chakra is. Thank and honor yourself. Bow in reverence to the love, light, wisdom, and power that *is* you and lives within you. Ask for whatever needs to be revealed to you to be revealed. Be aware. Tune in to your heart. Feel. See. Hear.

Next, move with condor and fly up to the top center of your head, where the crown chakra is. Envision a cosmic light beam beginning to emanate from your crown and, along with condor, fly up through the sky and clouds, through the galaxies and stars, until your beam reaches into Source, the field of consciousness. You will know when you've connected with this place. Give highest reverence, thanks, and gratitude to Great Spirit. Ask that you receive down your cosmic light beam and into your being whatever messages, medicine, and guidance need to serve your highest, greatest, earthly good and the highest good of all. Be aware. See. Feel. Hear.

Fly with condor down your cosmic light beam, returning back to your physical body. Allow the energetic medicines and blessings of these connection points in the ground and sky to fully harmonize within you. Hold condor in your heart.

When you feel complete, slowly open your eyes.

SYMBOLISM IN SOUTH AMERICA

In ancient Inca culture in South America, condors represented the gods of the air that carried messages from the heavens. The word *condor* comes from *kuntur* in the Incan native language Quechua. The Mapuche people of South America refer to the condor as the "king of birds," and believe the bird to possess their culture's four cardinal virtues: leadership, justice, wisdom, and goodness.

"Ten years ago, I was invited to a transformative eagle and condor ceremony that was filled with beautiful prayers and music. It was a powerful manifestation of the Eagle and Condor Prophecy, when the people of the north and south share traditions and pray with each other to balance the energies and weave healing energy into the human collective consciousness.

"Soon after this ceremony I received an unexpected job offer in Hawai'i and flew halfway across the world to start a new life. Six months later, I felt called back to New York. I had no money and no concrete plan, but I trusted my intuition and returned on a beautiful weekend of ceremonies with Navajo Elders. As I integrated the teachings and blessings from that healing weekend, I felt compelled to pick up my guitar and seamlessly played a beautiful melody that came through me, "Vuela Vuela Condorcito, Vuela Vuela con Dios." I feel this song is a beautiful representation of the condor energy: deeply intuitive, feminine, heart centered, and graceful, soaring high through the air with little effort. It doesn't need to hunt. It is provided for. It flies between the earthly and spiritual realms as a direct messenger to the Spirit.

"The condor brings medicine into our life when we work with its powerful energy, its connection to the true strength and beauty of our heart. The condor teaches us that when we prioritize the Spirit in our life, and trust and listen to our intuition, life flows and you are tapped into the courage and strength needed to fly into the unknown."

—Daniel Ceballos

SACRED SONG CARRIER

COYOTE

FEARLESSNESS • TRUTH • REVELATION • ILLUMINATION •
CLARITY FROM TRICKERY • PARADOX

WHEN TO WORK WITH ME:

When you want to see through illusion, when you want to drop the mask you've been wearing, when you're ready for truth to be revealed, when you're ready to let go of victim mentality

ENERGY MEDICINE:

Are you tricking yourself? Do you want things to be a certain way so badly that you are lying to yourself about reality? My medicine will help you get real and honest with yourself.

I am here to help you pause and ask yourself, "Where am I ignoring the teachings that are trying to present in my life? What wisdom is trying to get my attention, but I am turning a blind eye to?"

Know that no matter what decision you make you will be gifted with new wisdom, one way or another.

Are you able to maintain your center and calm when chaos presents? If not, it's time to do more inner work and build up the ability to trust yourself. This is key.

Rather than view yourself as a victim, can you begin to view what you experience from a place of fascination, learning, and awe? Take what is presenting and allow it to lift you through the lessons.

My throat and heart chakra medicine comes through howling. It returns you to your true, wild nature. Remember.

POWER PRACTICE:

In this practice, you'll howl at the full moon. It may feel strange at first, but this practice will activate deep medicine by letting you release inhibitions and allowing your mind, body, spirit, and soul to be *free*. On the full moon, find a place where you can safely be outside at night—the roof of your building, your backyard, a campsite—ideally a place where you can see the full moon. Tilt your head back and let yourself howl. Feel the vibrations in your throat. Let your true nature activate. Hold nothing back. When you're done, make time to meditate on or journal about how it made you feel and whether any ideas or thoughts revealed themselves when you gave yourself permission to *be free*.

THE CREATION OF THE STARS

The word coyote comes from the word "coyōtl" in the Nahuatl language spoken in Central America. Huehuecoyotl, which means "very old coyote," is a god of music, merriment, and storytelling in Aztec mythology. Huehuecoyotl possesses shape-shifting abilities and, like other Aztec deities, has a balance of dark and light attributes, representing duality. Also known as the prankster, Huehuecoyotl's deep wisdom paired with mischief and boredom can sometimes result in cruel tricks. But Huehuecoyotl is also known for passionately helping humans in need.

CRAB

SENSITIVITY • GUARDEDNESS • EMOTIONAL • HOUSEKEEPING • NEW DIRECTIONS • INTROVERSION

WHEN TO WORK WITH ME:

When you need to move past an obstacle, when you're ready to let love in, when you want to revamp your home, when you want to embrace your sensitivities and emotions more, when you're ready to satiate curiosities, when you're ready to explore and transform

ENERGY MEDICINE:

Have you been guarding your emotions in an attempt to protect yourself? Ask yourself whether you're pushing people and experiences away because you fear being hurt. How can you let love in?

It's OK to honor and embrace your sensitivities. Yes, you may feel to the deepest depths of your emotions, but this is a gift of being alive. In times of deep emotional discomfort, observe that energy and speak to it.

Remember that there are many paths to one goal. If the direction you have been taking has too much resistance, pause and consider a new path. Proceed in a different way around the obstruction.

Now is the time to trust yourself to handle all that comes your way.

I remind you that your physical space is important to tend to. Go through your home and clear out the items that are no longer serving you. Move things around to create new energy. Your home is your sanctuary.

It's time for some transformation. What curiosity has your soul been longing to explore? This is the moment to heed the call.

POWER PRACTICE:

When a crab outgrows its shell, it sheds its too-small home and creates a new one. In this meditation practice, you'll take an honest look at whether you've outgrown your current way of living. Staying in your secure shell may be enticing, but what feels like familiar comfort is actually preventing you from receiving the profound gifts of growth, expansion, and connection.

Close your eyes and connect with your breath and your heart. Once you feel centered, meditate on the following questions:

- Is my fear of being hurt closing me off to new experiences?
- Where in my life can I expand into greater joy and connection?
- Am I ready to allow myself to be supported, held, and loved?
- Am I willing to open myself up to expansion?

Once you've spent some time answering these questions, visualize a gorgeous shell next to you. It's a touch bigger than you are, with room for you to grow into it. Envision yourself stepping into this new home, filled with the energetic blessings and medicine that will fully support and empower your expansion.

A DIVINATION TOOL

For diviners among the Kapsiki and Higi people of present-day Cameroon and Nigeria, crabs were used to predict the future or read meaning into an unclear message. It is said that the diviners would recite special chants to connect with the crabs, which were then left to freely walk their path on the sand. The patterns in the sand created by the crabs, or the manner in which the crab walked, determined the messages.

CRICKET

DESIRABLE OUTCOMES • GOOD FORTUNE • MYSTICAL SONG • FREQUENCY RAISING • COURAGEOUS NEW HEIGHTS • INTEGRITY • DIVINE DISCERNMENT

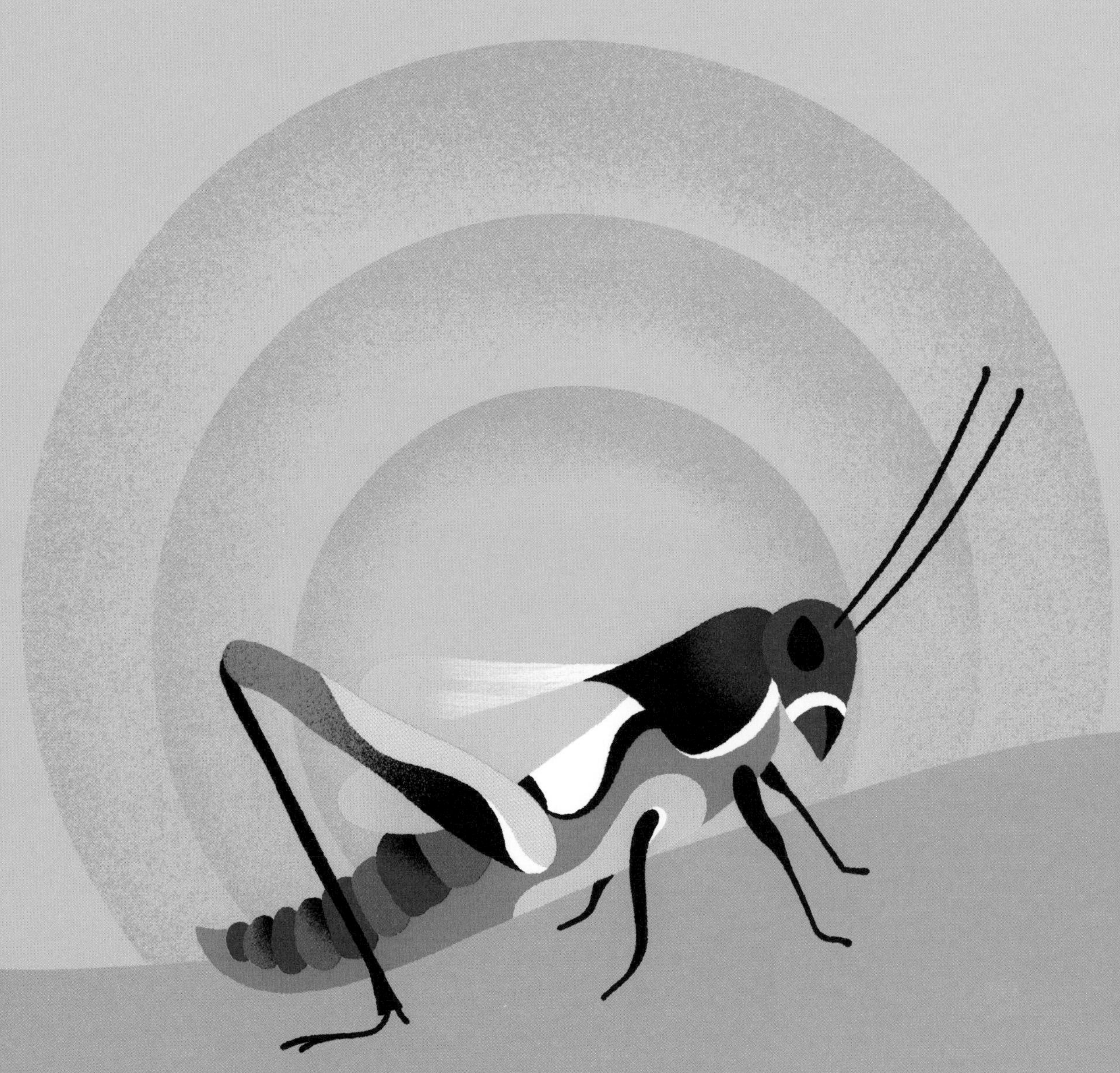

WHEN TO WORK WITH ME:

When you want to seize big opportunities, when you want to express your soul's purpose, when you want to open your heart, when you need clarity on decisions, when you want to be filled with integrity, when you want high vibrations

ENERGY MEDICINE:

I am known for my voice and song. I help you find your voice and discover your unique song.

I am a protector of what is positive. Call upon me to bring forward a vibration-lifting experience in your life.

Transparency and integrity are my main medicines. I am here to remind you that it is better to be honest and real. Transparency is clear energy and provides a clear path. Manipulation and delusions create fog, chaos, and distortion. Staying true to what you know is right will always provide unexpected miracles.

I can help awaken your spiritual gifts, like dream analysis, chakra healing, aura or energy readings, and more. Call upon me when you're ready to connect to your spiritual potential.

Are you expressing your heart? Are you holding back on love? Remember your true power and greatest guidance system live in your heart center; don't let them lay dormant.

Now is a ripe time of higher possibilities for you. What is presenting in your life that you should take the leap toward?

POWER PRACTICE:

In this practice, you will connect with cricket's song medicine. Sit nice and tall with your spine erect, close your eyes, connect with your breath, and call upon cricket to join you in ceremony. Hear the sound of its chirping song in your head. Now, give yourself full permission to start singing or using your voice in whatever way your spirit is called to. Allow the sounds to emanate from you in any way they come out; don't edit or hold back. Let yourself be open, free, and uninhibited. If you have a drum, rattle, or other instrument on hand, bring that into the song. This practice is simply about letting your voice and the sounds of your soul be heard, in whatever form they wish, with no judgment or pretense. Once you've completed this practice, thank cricket and ask it to remain with you in bringing your true song to the world.

A PET ALARM

During the Tang dynasty in China, it was fairly common for people to keep crickets in small cages. The insects acted as a sort of alarm system: Their singing was a sign that all was safe and good. If a stranger came to the house during the night, the cricket stopped singing. The sudden silence was a warning that someone was approaching who did not belong to the household.

CROW

OMEN OF CHANGE • PERSONAL INTEGRITY • WALK YOUR TALK •
THE VOID • CREATION • MAGIC

WHEN TO WORK WITH ME:

When you are ready to trust your personal integrity, when you want to align with your power during times of great change or uncertainty, when you are ready to birth a new project or way of living, when you need spiritual strength

ENERGY MEDICINE:

I am a very potent shamanic totem. I represent Great Spirit and the birth point of creation.

I reveal the magic that is ever present. My call urges you to leave what is familiar and see your life from a higher perspective.

When you ask for my medicine, I help you transcend judgments and concepts of "right" and "wrong."

I give you strength when you are dealing with any type of adversity, as I can show you how to rise above and stay strong.

I also represent great transformation. What needs changing in your life? Be honest with yourself.

Know that you have many untapped abilities waiting for you. Explore your gifts and call to me for support.

POWER PRACTICE:

Crow represents the void, the home of infinite possibilities and miracles. In this practice, you will enter the void. Find a quiet place to sit comfortably with your eyes closed. Envision yourself walking toward a golden door. As you get closer and closer, feel the beautiful energies emanating from the door. Turn the golden doorknob, and step through the door into a completely black abyss. Release yourself into this space. Allow your body to do what it wants, whether that's lying on your back feeling the support of the Universe or moving your arms as you swim through the void. Do what you're guided to do.

Once you've settled into the experience of the abyss, call forward the energetic medicine of the void—a place of infinite possibility—to fuel your highest earthly good and let it enter in. Ask the void whether it has any messages for you and receive the answers. Trust whatever comes up.

Now you can begin to swim or float back to the golden door. Once you're at the doorway, turn back to the void and feel how this space has fully supported you. Thank the void for welcoming and empowering you. Once you've finished, exit through the doorway and shut the door behind you.

Back on the Earth plane, feel your body connected fully to the ground and call yourself back to your physical body. Breathe gratitude into your heart, gently open your eyes, and return to your physical space.

Remember that on the other side of suffering or spiritual stagnation, the void is always there, ready to welcome you.

"The Suquamish people of the Pacific Northwest you were thinking or speaking about when you crow, stop and reflect upon what you've just been ing with someone else. Crows are monogamous. ships, which is very much a human requirement which is also part of the epigenetics of how human between the crow world and the human world. dismantling the inner structure of bigotry and issues, and economic, political, and religious collectors. We need to collect people of all colors, equals. We need to collect people with different structures and spiritual attitudes. We need to be have a saying that you should 'remember what hear the crow calling.' Whenever you hear the thinking or what you've just been communicat- They respond to the reflective nature of relation- as well. Crows have a way of transferring memory, DNA works. There are a lot of alignments The crow is a collector. Right now, humans are phobia, in racial issues, sexual issues, gender issues. We need to be like the crows and be sexual orientations, and genders together as politics and economics, different religious collectors, like the crows."

—Guru Singh
YOGA MASTER

DEER

PATH OF THE OPEN HEART • GENTLE STRENGTH • UNCONDITIONAL LOVE • GREATEST DIVINE EMBRACE • KINDNESS • COMPASSION • SERENITY

WHEN TO WORK WITH ME:

When you want your heart to heal or open, when you want to inspire through kindness rather than force, when you want to give and receive unconditional love, when you want to stop being so hard on yourself or others.

ENERGY MEDICINE:

I teach of gentleness and heart intelligence, but do not mistake these qualities for weaknesses. Work with my medicine and you will learn the potent power of fierce grace.

If you are in need of softening, healing, or expanding your heart, look no further. My medicine is here for you always, to guide you back home to your heart, knowing it is safe to love, time and time again.

Have you been too harsh or critical? Remember to be tender and compassionate with yourself and others. It is safe to trust the path of vulnerability, speaking and acting from the heart.

Do you know that there is strength in gentleness? Have you tried this way of living before? Being open to this experience may be the greatest decision of your life.

If you have been hurt by another, call me forward to tend to your beautiful heart. Allow me to whisper my messages into it and support it in its healing so it can remain open to love again.

Wherever you are heading in life, whatever you're currently achieving, is it being done from a place of positive intentions? Working with me helps you get clear-hearted, the ideal state to be in as you move toward your dreams.

POWER PRACTICE:

Deer can migrate hundreds of miles, jumping over obstacles, wading through water, and crossing endless hills. Deer shows us how to navigate the varying experiences of our lives with agility and forward momentum. In this practice, you will investigate how you navigate the rolling terrain of your experiences—are you moving forward with an expansive, open heart, or are you shutting down?

Find a quiet place to sit with your journal and pen and answer "yes" or "no" to the following questions.

- Am I willing to do the necessary work to heal or further expand my heart?
- Do I trust myself to set healthy boundaries?
- Do I love and honor myself with tenderness and compassion?
- Have I attended to past rifts that require forgiveness or healing?
- Am I willing to act with vulnerability?

Now look back through your answers and spend a few minutes journaling about what you've learned. Consider how you can keep your heart open and tender as you navigate the path ahead. Call on deer to help you move through these experiences with more agility.

THE DEER IN BUDDHISM

The deer is among the earliest and most important symbols of Buddhism. It was in Deer Park at Sarnath that Gautama Buddha preached his first sermon and "turned the wheel of the Law," which revealed the doctrines of reincarnation and karma. Deer are often depicted in Buddhist art as attending Buddha, usually kneeling near the base of the lotus where the Great Teacher sat.

"The deer has always been in my life. Growing up on an acreage outside the city, deer were regular visitors to our property. I remember seeing how deer could guide their young with such compassion and love, and then turn around and chase off a coyote with courage and deep strength. Whenever possible, I would take walks out into the bush to try and find antler sheds—a gift from the deer. It wasn't until I started my shamanic training that I began to learn just how powerful the deer is. In my training, I learned that the deer could help me shed what was becoming a burden, much like how they shed their antlers. The deer also taught me that it is important to walk softly on the Earth and to take care of our planet, and ultimately ourselves.

"The most profound experiences I have had with deer actually don't have anything to do with me. Deer will always make herself known during a healing session when my client is in need of that sweet, gentle, motherly energy. Healing can sometimes be fast and intense, but deer helps my clients move gently through their healing. Deer will always find a way to get an antler to my client when they are in need of this type of healing. Last year, I was working with a client in my downtown home. Halfway through the session, I happened to look out my window to the alley and could see a striking, white object lying on the ground. I moved closer to the window and saw it was a perfectly white antler sitting there, waiting to be seen. How did it get to an alley in the middle of the city? Well, that's up to deer. The antler went on to become a powerful healing tool for my client."

—Garrett McCoy

HEALER AND ENERGY MEDICINE PRACTITIONER

INTELLIGENCE • JOY • HIGH-LEVEL COMMUNICATION • BREATH • WATER AND AIR • STRESS RELIEF • EMOTIONAL INTEGRATION

WHEN TO WORK WITH ME:

When you want to clear old emotions, when you want to be more playful, when you want to communicate, when you want to connect with your mystical gifts, when you want to activate your intelligence, when you want to experience greater ease, when you want to access the ancient wisdoms inside of you

ENERGY MEDICINE:

I remind you to feel your emotions. Allow them to inform and teach you. Do not fear the more challenging emotions, but rather honor them, ask them questions, and allow them to integrate so you become more whole.

Are you making things harder than necessary? How open are you to allowing more joy, harmony, love, and play into your life? Struggle doesn't need to be a normal part of life; let things come with ease.

I am always your ally, taking you to the true mystical essence of who you are and healing any wounded part of you in a loving way.

I evoke ancient remembrance. Connect with me and see whether you can feel, see, or recall ancient wisdom truths of long ago inside you.

Telepathic spiritual gifts are my specialty. Call upon me to strengthen your ability to communicate with others and your spiritual guides simply by transmitting the directed communication through thought.

I embody medicine of very strong intelligence. Work with me to function and communicate on a high level.

POWER PRACTICE:

When you feel stress, concern, or other difficult emotions beginning to take over, call on the healing power of dolphin to help you release tension through your breath. Find a place to sit quietly and bow to honor the emotion. Acknowledge the emotion, as it is simply trying to communicate and help you get into alignment. Then ask the emotion, "Dear ____ (sadness, anger, frustration, etc.), what do you want me to know? Why are you revealing to me? What do you need in order to let go?" Spend time with these questions until you've received answers, and then call dolphin in to work with you. Sit up tall with your spine straight, close your eyes, and begin to connect with your breath. Focus on the emotion you are ready to clear as you inhale through your nose. Hold your breath for 4 seconds as you focus the emotion you're releasing. Then, as you visualize dolphin powerfully releasing water from its blowhole, open your mouth and release your difficult emotion in a strong, forceful exhale. Repeat this breathwork sequence at least four times or until you feel the emotion clear.

APOLLO, THE DOLPHIN

In Greek mythology, the god Apollo once took the form of a dolphin in order to force a crew of sailors to move to a temple city he'd established. Disguised as a dolphin, Apollo leapt aboard a ship and steered it to the city of Crisa. Once there, Apollo revealed himself as a god and initiated the sailors into his service, with directions to pray to him as Apollo or Delphinos, meaning "dolphin," from which Crisa received its new name: Delphi.

"When I was pregnant with my first son, a Maori Elder put his hand on my pregnant belly and said, 'Very powerful boy you are having. Call him Eka.' Eka is the dolphin spirit who takes the spirit of the dead to the underworld and back to the light through a portal in the North Island of New Zealand.

"When I met my partner, he had a medicine wheel with two dolphins swimming in a sea of sacred geometry with infinity signs and love hearts. He had been using it to call in his soul mate, and along I came, pregnant with Eka.

"When I was pregnant with our second son, we visited a place in Australia called Monkey Mia, where dolphins come up to the shore to interact with humans. Aboriginal people who once lived in the area formed a relationship with the dolphins, who helped them fish and, in return, the people fed the dolphins some of their catch. We learned there was a cave along the coastline where Aboriginal women would go to give birth.

"We walked down the beach and played music. Soon, the dolphins came to check us out. I got in the water and a huge dolphin came up to me. I squatted down so she could use her sonar to see I was pregnant. I felt her telepathically communicate to me to touch her belly. I touched her, and to my joy, I felt a baby move and realized she too was pregnant. I have a huge C-section scar across my belly from my first birth (Eka was breech, and we later realized dolphins birth tail first) and the pregnant dolphin placed her beak smack in the middle of my scar. I reckon she sent healing light into it.

"Later, when it came time for me to give birth, I labored in a bathtub, wearing a mask and snorkel so I could lie facedown to alleviate the pain. Suddenly, I was transported to the ocean. I saw the dolphin from Monkey Mia. She was in labor and she sent out a signal to all the female dolphins, who came and circled her as she birthed her baby. I witnessed the tail slip out and then the precious baby dolphin. The auntie dolphins swam in and lifted the baby dolphin to the surface to take its first breath while the mother birthed the placenta. It was as clear as if I were there. Seventeen hours later, my second son, Hopi Lawin—the peaceful eagle—slipped out into the warm waters of our birthing pool.

"I know beyond a shadow of a doubt that dolphins and I go way back to ancient times. I only need to think of them, and they appear wherever I am at the ocean. We feel each other, like old friends."

—Malaika MaVeena Darville

SHAMANIC MEDICINE WOMAN

DRAGONFLY

ADAPTABILITY • MYSTICISM AND MAGIC • WATER •
EASE • GRACE • TRUTH

WHEN TO WORK WITH ME:

When you want more ease and grace in your life, when you're ready for a swift change and don't want to resist it, when you want to break free of old patterns holding you back, when you want to shift past an old mentality or way of thinking, when you're ready to release suffering and activate more lightheartedness into your life

ENERGY MEDICINE:

Call upon me to see truth in a situation.

I remind you that there is mysticism and multidimension in everything. Call upon me when you want to connect more with the supernatural, the support of nature, and the elemental world (plants, air, earth, fire, and water).

I possess great compassion and assist with any healing or counseling work.

I help you tune in to and evoke more lightheartedness and joy in your life.

I will release your rigidity and allow you to shape-shift, quickly change directions, and transform.

Call upon me to break old patterns that are not serving you.

What is your deepest desire and what outcome do you want? I will help you follow this path with ease.

POWER PRACTICE:

Dragonfly is one of the most colorful species on the planet, and it can bring vibrant energy to your life. To work with this animal, you will connect with the elements of air and water. First, make time to go outside and find a place you can sit quietly—it could be your backyard, a balcony, or a local park. Feel the air on your skin and notice the quality of the temperature, the wind. Receive its energy and messages. Give thanks for this substance that gives us life.

To connect with water, take a healing bath. Add Epsom salts and any crystals or herbs that are safe for use in water and soak for at least 15 minutes, enjoying this moment of ease and allowing your auric field to be cleared. (If you don't have access to a bathtub, you can do this in the shower, gently scrubbing your body with salt.) Imagine the weight of any stress or pressure washing off your shoulders and be light. Feel your energy being lifted.

"When I was five years old, some kids were playing outside our apartment with a dragonfly tied on a string. One of its wings was broken. When I yelled for my abuelita, the kids ran off and I carefully brought the pieces of the dead dragonfly into the house. My dad told me that tying a string to a dragonfly and flying it like a kite was a common pastime for kids. But it didn't seem like a pastime to me. I found it deeply upsetting.

"I've felt connected to the dragonfly since that day. By the time I was a teenager, I saw dragonflies everywhere. I saw them printed on T-shirts, painted on buildings, and flying outdoors. I decided that dragonflies would represent a sign that I was going in the right direction. Anytime I had to make a big life decision, I asked a dragonfly to show herself. I'd say, 'If this is right, then I'll see a dragonfly so I know I'm going the right way.'

"Before I quit my job to become a yoga teacher, I was struggling to find fulfillment. I was lost and knew I wasn't living my purpose. I went for a drive with the windows down. I stopped at a light and just as I was thinking about quitting my job, a dragonfly flew into my car through the window and back out. I was shocked. It happened so quickly that my first thought was, 'This is nothing.' Then, a different dragonfly entered and did the exact same thing! That's all it took. I quit my job the next day, and I haven't looked back since."

—Rosie Acosta

YOGA AND MEDITATION TEACHER AND AUTHOR

DUCK

SENSE OF HUMOR • STEADINESS IN THE STORMS • SPIRITUAL CAPABILITIES • EMOTIONAL WELL-BEING • MARRIAGE • PLAYFULNESS

WHEN TO WORK WITH ME:

When you want to connect with your emotions, when you want to step into your spiritual gifts, when you want to lead or teach, when you don't want to get pulled into other people's drama, when you want to call forward sacred partnership, when you want to be more playful

ENERGY MEDICINE:

I work with the power of emotions. Is there a particular emotion you find yourself resisting in life? Know that every emotion has deep wisdom and fuel to share with us; it's simply a matter of asking them and inquiring what they're revealing to teach us.

I remind you not to fear your spiritual capabilities. You can trust that your highest self has chosen to incarnate with certain gifts that would always serve you, so don't be afraid to let them come alive.

Have you been feeling the itch to lead or guide? Tune in to your innate ability to empower others and add positive energy to the community. See where your services are needed.

While my legs and feet may be feverishly paddling under the water, above the surface I appear to glide along with total ease. Keep your emotional center and power.

Remember, you do not need to get pulled into other people's energies and situations.

I remind you to play and have fun. What can you do today that awakens your sense of joy and wonder?

One of my strongest medicinal attributes pertains to joyful relationships and marriages. Call upon me to further strengthen a current partnership or to call in a most special one.

POWER PRACTICE:

If you're seeking a harmonious relationship, place a drawing, a photograph, or figurines of two ducks in a sacred place, like the altar in your home or on your nightstand. In your daily prayer or meditation, call upon the medicine of duck to reveal anything you need to do within yourself to reach your own personal sovereignty. In order to be in healthy partnership, you first need to actualize and embody complete personal power and wholeness within yourself. When you land in this place of independence, you will be ready to show up fully in a sacred union. Be devoted, open, and willing to have these inner conversations with yourself, with duck by your side, and know deep down that committing to cultivating your own personal power will lead to rewarding partnership.

A SYMBOL OF A HAPPY UNION

In Chinese and Japanese cultures, the mandarin duck is an ancient symbol of marital fidelity, happiness, and devotion, as it was believed this type of duck remained in partnership for life. Korean cultures also look to the mandarin duck for harmony in marriage, sometimes incorporating a pair of duck carvings into wedding ceremonies.

EAGLE

DIVINE MESSENGER • PRAYER • HIGHEST VISION • COURAGE • SEXUAL ENERGY • HIDDEN TRUTHS • STRENGTH • NONATTACHMENT

WHEN TO WORK WITH ME:

When you need a healthier or broader perspective, when you want more freedom and independence, when you want to get in touch with your sexuality, when you want to practice nonattachment, when you want to see through falsehoods and have effective communication

ENERGY MEDICINE:

If you are feeling foggy or confused, pause, breathe, and call upon me to provide a broader perspective. Trust yourself and move forward with strength.

Be wise, clear, connected, and concise with your speech. Speak few words, fully grounded in power, to express yourself.

Nonattachment is a main medicine of mine. When you tune in to the trust in yourself and the Universe, you do not need to grip so tightly to things. Allow yourself to be in faith and flow.

Do you feel free? Free to express and be loved, free to be who you truly are, free to share your gifts with the world, free to experience abundance and joy? Liberation is calling to you.

I represent reverence and nobility for walking the spiritual path. Now is the time to engage in spiritual devotion and commitments.

When I present to you, Great Spirit is trying to get your attention. What signs have been coming in from the universe? It's time to tune in.

POWER PRACTICE:

Eagle's large talons—four on each foot—have a powerful grip. In this practice, you'll connect with the image of the talons to represent holding onto your dreams as you soar toward new heights. In your journal, draw eagle's foot with four large talons. Beneath each one, write down one positive thing you are ready to experience in life. Remember, eagle is the highest vision and messenger of Spirit—don't hold back in what you are ready for. Place this piece of paper on your altar or a sacred space in your home. In the morning, light a candle next to the image and close your eyes, envisioning each positive experience and the feelings that will come with it. Ask eagle to come to you and reveal what next steps you need to take to have these dreams manifest.

DAY AND NIGHT

The eagle is revered by various Native North American cultures, including the Abenaki tribe. In their tradition, Kisosen is a solar deity symbolized as an eagle, whose name literally means "Sun-Bringer." This tradition holds that the day is created when the eagle's wings open and the night is created when its wings close.

POWERFUL VISION

Aligning with its energy medicine of possessing highest vision, the eagle can see four to five times better than humans. Their eyes are angled 30 degrees away from the center of their face, giving them a wider field of view, and they can see five colors (versus our three) and detect UV light.

"The eagle came into my life when my brother transcended this life. I experienced a depth of sadness and acceptance I hadn't known before. Several people I had been working with for years let me know that I was visiting their dreams with the eagle. There were a few bald eagles where I was staying, and they were present with me during these months.

"The week that my brother transitioned, I was able to sit in a healing space with a woman who carries the frog spirit medicine. While I was on that shamanic journey, I saw my brother and my guides standing around an operating table. My brother looked frightened and spoke to a guide I had never seen, who was an Eagle Woman. He said, 'If you take it out, she may die.' The Eagle Woman said, 'Let her decide.' As I drew closer, I saw myself on the operating table. The spirit was operating on my heart, removing a shard that had been lodged there my whole life. I dropped into that body and was no longer the observer. I opened my eyes and said, 'I want to live.' I was stunned to see that the Eagle Woman was me as I am now, covered in white eagle feathers.

"The eagle has been present in my prayers, dreams, and meditations ever since. The eagle is a messenger and carrier of prayers. Eagle has taught me to be a good listener to the message beyond what is said. As a healer, I am helped by eagle to hear a person's true prayer, even when they don't have the words to communicate what their soul's dream is for this lifetime. Eagle has brought me courage, strength, tenacity, and timing, and reminded me to keep my mind in my purest and highest prayer for life. Eagle has made me more honest and willing to let go and observe trials with love and detachment."

—Nicole Adriana Casanova
SACRED ACTIVIST

ELEPHANT

INCREDIBLE WISDOM • KINDNESS • SEXUAL POWER • HAPPINESS • FAMILY • REMOVING OBSTACLES • REGALITY • SENSE OF SMELL

WHEN TO WORK WITH ME:

When you want to connect with family, when you want to unlock your ancient wisdom, when you want to be more likable, when you want to be more adventurous sexually, when you want to remove blocks, when you want more self-honor

ENERGY MEDICINE:

I represent regality and royalty. What does being treated with honor, respect, and dignity look and feel like to you?

I am known for my incredible sense of smell. I remind you to make decisions based on what smells good or smells bad to you. When making a choice, speak it out loud and ask yourself, "If I say yes to this, does that smell sweet or rotten?" Heed the answer.

I have the powerful ability to remove obstacles for you. If you feel like you are ready to transcend blocks standing in the way of your greatness, call upon me to work with you in these processes.

Protection, loyalty, and standing up for others all live within my medicinal strengths.

I remind you to treat others with care and kindness, like family. Is there someone who could benefit from your care right now?

I embody strong but compassionate leadership. How can you apply these abilities in your own personal or professional life?

POWER PRACTICE:

Elephant represents strong sensual power and sense of smell, so in this practice, you'll explore connecting with your body using meditation and alluring scents. Collect essential oils and ingredients that appeal to you, including your favorite flowers, organic oils, and scented candles. Light the candles, surround yourself with flowers, and use the oil on your skin or in a diffuser. Sit in meditation with your eyes closed and ask yourself what sacred sensual experience your soul is yearning for. As you sit, run your hands over your skin, sending love to your physical body. Know that you are deserving of joy and affection.

REMOVER OF OBSTACLES

In Hinduism, Lord Ganesh is an elephant-headed god known as the remover of obstacles, Lord of Beginnings, and the Deity of Good Fortune. Before any sacred rituals or ceremonies, Ganesh mantras are chanted to bring protection, prosperity, and power and remove any possible blocks that may lie ahead physically or energetically.

FERRET

EXPLORATION OF SELF AND OTHERS • SURPLUS • ENERGY • SECRETS OR SURPRISE • STEALTH • CYCLES OF LIFE • NEGOTIATION

WHEN TO WORK WITH ME:

When you're involved in negotiations, when you need to sniff out truths, when you need to restore, when you want abundant supplies, when you're ready to take responsibility, when you want to process surprising information, when you need to be reminded that all is sacred

ENERGY MEDICINE:

I am a reminder for you to take inventory and set aside an extra supply of anything that could support you in the future. Mindful, abundant storage is the name of my game.

I represent various life cycles, whether that is the shadow and light we all possess, death and rebirth, or yin and yang. Remember that all is sacred, and all is our great teacher.

I am sly, clever, and smart. Don't fool yourself into believing things that you know are not true. What truths have you been ignoring in your life?

Now may be a good time for you to momentarily retreat into a space where you feel cozy, supported, and held.

I carry with me the medicines of secrets and surprise. If you have learned something that feels shocking to your system, call on me to ground you and open your mind to new horizons in a healthy way.

I am all about taking responsibility for your life and what you choose to experience. Earthly lessons can oftentimes feel challenging, but remember, we call into our lives what we need to learn so we can grow. Victim energy keeps you small. Taking ownership will help you expand.

POWER PRACTICE:

Ferrets are known for burrowing into comfy covens, so tune in to ferret's energy to create a spot in your home that supports your healing work—what I like to call a "healing haven." Find a quiet place where you can make your own supportive and cozy ferret nook. It could be the corner of your bedroom, or even a closet. Once the spot is designated, place a few special items in this area that evoke feelings of total warmth, being held, and being loved. Consider items like a soft blanket and meditation pillow, candles, feathers or other spiritual tools, and essential oils. This is your space to retreat whenever you're in need of comfort or healing. Visit this space as often as you need, especially any time you are having an awakening or feeling the intense emotions that come with bravely facing what needs to be faced.

FLAMINGO

BALANCE • FUN • EMOTIONAL INTELLIGENCE • OPENHEARTEDNESS • DEDICATION TO FAMILY AND FRIENDS

WHEN TO WORK WITH ME:

When you need to find balance, when you need to let loose, when you need to spend time with or appreciate your friends and family more, when you need an emotional healing or clearing, when you want to open your heart

ENERGY MEDICINE:

My main medicine is balance. Is there an area of your life that is untended to and another area where you're focusing too much of your precious energy? Take an honest inventory, and then invite me to help restore better balance.

I am here to remind you to lighten up, be more carefree, and have some fun.

Have you been playing small? Going along with what someone else wants more than what you and your intuition want? Stand tall and remember the bright and unique essence that you are.

I represent strong emotions. If you've been riding some big emotions lately, do your best to celebrate that rollercoaster. Your ability to feel is the gift of being alive.

I am also here to remind you not to fear the power of your heart and all the love you have inside. This is one of your greatest gifts, so do not close your heart from those willing and open to receiving.

When was the last time you expressed your gratitude to your family and friends? It's important that those in your life feel important, seen, and appreciated.

POWER PRACTICE:

Flamingo's main medicine is balance, and this balancing breathwork and meditation practice will help you introduce more harmony between the elements of your life.

Find a place to sit comfortably. Keep your spine straight and close your eyes. Take deep, slow breaths in the following rhythm: breathe in for 4 seconds, hold your breath for 4 seconds, exhale for 4 seconds, hold your breath for 4 seconds. Repeat the sequence for at least 2 minutes or until you feel centered, present, and calm.

Now envision yourself as a flamingo covered in bright pink feathers. Feel your wings flapping and begin to lift off the ground. Notice the quality of your flight, how you find gentle balance as you ride the breeze. Now imagine a beautiful beach below, where you gently land. There, you're greeted by a beautiful flamingo who asks you three questions:

- What goals, relationships, or experiences are you ready to give more attention to?
- Where can you release some time and energy in your life?
- What will things look like when these elements are in better balance?

Once you've answered each question, thank your flamingo friend and open your eyes. Spend a few minutes considering what was illuminated in your conversation with the flamingo. How you can commit to finding a healthier balance in your life?

COMMUNITY IS KEY

Aligned with its energy medicine that represents relationships with friends and family, flamingos are known to live in very large groups. Their cooperation is exhibited in the way they build, protect, and nurture their nests together. The largest flock of flamingos ever recorded—more than 1 million—was found in Lake Bogoria, Kenya.

FLY

DETERMINATION • PERSISTENCE • FLEXIBILITY • SELF-CENTERING • SURVIVAL • ALCHEMY

WHEN TO WORK WITH ME:

When you need to complete a project or goal, when you need to release victim mentality, when you need to turn hardship into gold, when you need to find the path of least resistance, when you need to clear your life of negativity

ENERGY MEDICINE:

You work hard to reach your goals. I remind you that while it may feel selfish to take the time and energy you need to cross the finish line, sometimes you have to honor the path of your goal and do what you need to do.

Remember that your mission and goals will most likely not be as important to others as they are to you. If support is needed to actualize the goal, risk peskiness for the manifestation of the bigger dream.

If you're feeling stuck, ask yourself how you can adapt and change course to achieve. What negative energy can you remove from your life? Take an honest look at any people or situations that are toxic, dysfunctional, or weighing you down. Clear your path to thriving.

Do not allow challenges to deter you. Anything and everything can be alchemized (turned into love and power to ascend you). Hardships happen to teach and amplify hidden strengths and gifts.

I remind you that in your pursuits, while self-importance may be a key temporarily, this path warns of turning to narcissism and overstepping boundaries if not walked with humility and grace.

POWER PRACTICE:

In this practice, you'll tap into fly energy to clear any negativity blocking your progress. Begin by taking out your journal or a piece of paper. Think of a goal you *really* want to accomplish. Write it down at the top of the page. Now draw a line down the middle of the page below your goal. On the left side of the line, write down any negative things you tell yourself about why it's too hard to move forward or why you won't achieve your goal.

Now, call upon fly to join you and activate your inner power and persistence. Close your eyes for a moment and tune in to your experience with flies. Picture them flying around relentlessly, doing what they need to do to get what they want. No matter how many times you swat at them, they come back again and again and seem unbothered by your attempts to make them go away. They're determined and persistent. Now, open your eyes. Harnessing that fly energy, ask yourself, "When I am in my full power, how do I feel? How do I carry myself? How can I respond to my own self-doubts? How do I stay as persistent as the fly when the world throws obstacles in my way?" Jot down your thoughts on the right side of the page. Now gaze over your two lists, and remind yourself that when the items in the left column arise, you can tune in to the right column to connect with the power of the fly and can stay persistent on the path to achieving your dreams.

FOX

SHAPE-SHIFTING • ATTUNEMENT • RESOURCEFULNESS • STEALTH • WISDOM • SOLUTIONS • HUMOR • MAGIC • INVISIBILITY • DREAMS

WHEN TO WORK WITH ME:

When you need clever solutions or smart ideas, when you need clear insight before making a decision, when you want to properly assess your surroundings and relationships, when you need more humor in your life, when you want to understand messages in your dreams

ENERGY MEDICINE:

I have nighttime powers. I enhance your ability to receive divine messages and creative inspiration at night and in your dreams.

I remind you to take a moment to attune to your surroundings before jumping into action. A pause, and practicing patience, will give you power.

Are you aware of your blind spots? Call upon me when you need to clearly see what to do, especially in areas of your life where historically you've made decisions that don't support your highest self.

When you're experiencing tension or anxiety, call upon me to ignite insight and intelligent decision-making in order to help you get to a higher-vibrational plane.

I also possess trickster medicine—when you are faced with tricky situations or people who may be deceiving you, I am your greatest ally.

Have you been too serious lately? I remind you that humor and laughter are filled with wisdom and spirituality.

POWER PRACTICE:

This practice will clear negative energy and awaken playfulness and creativity. At night before you go to sleep, find a place to sit or lie comfortably. Close your eyes and envision yourself as a sly, smart fox weaving your way through a forest in the dead of night. Feel how you nimbly navigate your way through the woods, using your keen eyes to avoid any obstacles as you move with quiet stealth and precision. Now begin to envision the trees as the things that bog you down and block your creativity—maybe it's obligations, or difficult relationships, or fear of failure. Continue to weave through the trees, confidently avoiding any trees in your way. Now begin to run, playfully bounding and darting through the night as you feel the fresh air move along your lithe fox body. Call upon the wisdom of the forest, Earth, and night sky to awaken in you a sense of playfulness and inspiration. Run for as long as you like, ending in a wide-open field lit by the moon. Finally, ask yourself, "What are the obstacles stopping me from approaching life with playfulness? How can I approach life more like fox?" Open your eyes and thank fox for showing you the way.

THE FOX IN TAROT

Staying true to its nighttime medicine, the fox is a central figure of the tarot card for the moon. It is often displayed as the route to the moon and the path of reincarnation.

FROG

WATER • HEALING • MOVING FORWARD • EMOTIONS • WEALTH • CLEANSING TOXICITY

WHEN TO WORK WITH ME:

When you're in need of emotional healing, when you're working with the element of water, when you need courage to move forward, when you want to allow in more wealth, when you want to open to new possibilities

ENERGY MEDICINE:

Water is one of my main medicines. If you are going through a time of great, deep change or experiencing toxicity in your life, utilize the miraculous power of bathing. Make a point to immerse in a healing bath, shower, or natural body of water and be held by the water medicine.

Your emotions may be intense, but I urge you to sit with them instead of pushing them away. You must honestly face your feelings in order to be able to navigate them in a healthy way. As they say, "You must feel it to heal it"—feel your deep emotions all the way through and then you can move ahead.

Along with water, I also work closely with the powers of the moon. To work with my energy, I recommend you partake in new and full moon rituals.

I remind you that you have the power to be in charge of your own environment, and my croaking song reminds you that finding your voice is key. Do not hold back. Sing, shout, or speak your truth.

Are you looking for a sign before you move forward? This is it. Take the leap in the direction you know will serve you best. Allow yourself to be open to a new world, perspective, or viewpoint. It's all happening now.

POWER PRACTICE:

In this practice, you'll work with frog's water and song energy to clear away any toxicity from your life and environment. This is especially useful if you're in, or emerging from, a time of upheaval. Choose a cleansing water or song ritual that calls to you. Maybe it's taking a bath with Epsom salts, walking in the rain, chanting, or singing a song. Whatever you choose, during the cleansing practice close your eyes and connect with your breath and heart chakra, the energy center in the middle of your chest. Once you feel centered and calmer, call frog forward. Imagine frog sitting in a pond of water, proudly croaking. Ask frog to clear you of any old emotional debris or toxicity that is no longer serving your greatest good. Feel frog's medicine washing over you. Thank frog for helping you cleanse your energy.

A REVERED AMPHIBIAN

Many global traditions highly revere the frog, including ancient Egypt, where frogs symbolized life and fertility because the Nile brings forth fertility to the barren lands and spawns millions of frogs. And in Chinese mythology, the frog is a female spirit (yin) and symbolizes healing and abundance. The frog was a favorite pet of the god of wealth, which was symbolized by golden or jade frog statues with coins on their lips.

GIRAFFE

CLAIRVOYANCE • CONNECTION BETWEEN EARTH AND SKY • MANIFESTATION OF HIGH VISIONS • GOING FOR IT

WHEN TO WORK WITH ME:

When you're ready to get unstuck or overcome whatever is holding you back, when you want to stop worrying, when you want to improve your personal relationships, when you want support to reach your highest dreams

ENERGY MEDICINE:

When you want to ground and manifest your visions, call upon me to be with you. I connect earth to sky.

Lift your head, stand tall, and walk in your power. I will support you in this.

To vibrate higher and release yourself from lower-vibration scenarios or people who are holding you back, work with my medicine in meditation.

Expand your view of what is possible for you and your life. I enhance your intuition and spiritual vision.

I bring a reminder to keep expanding courageously into the unknown. Living in this way will keep you more connected to the Universe and the wisdom within you. Do. Not. Settle.

I bring you grace and solid footing as you traverse your way through the school of life.

POWER PRACTICE:

Giraffe's medicine brings earthly manifestation to your highest visions. In this power practice, you'll check in with yourself and connect to the grandest visions for your life. Close your eyes and ask yourself what it is that you truly want to feel and experience—in your relationships, in your career, in your spiritual life. Then, open your eyes and create a vision board with pictures and words representing your highest visions. Place a picture of giraffe at the center of your vision board to ground the visions and assist in their manifestation. Place the board in your bedroom, somewhere you can see it every morning when you wake up and every night before you go to sleep.

LONG NECKS, BIG HEARTS

The giraffe's connection between earth and sky, and its courageous medicine are reflected in its impressive physical attributes. The tallest mammals on Earth, giraffes can reach up to 20 feet [6 m] in height once they are fully grown. They also have huge hearts. Literally. A giraffe's heart can be up to 2 feet [60 cm] long and weight up to 25 pounds [11 kg].

GNAT

CHANGE IN PERSPECTIVE • SHADOW WORK • COMFORT IN DISCOMFORT • HEEDING THE CALL

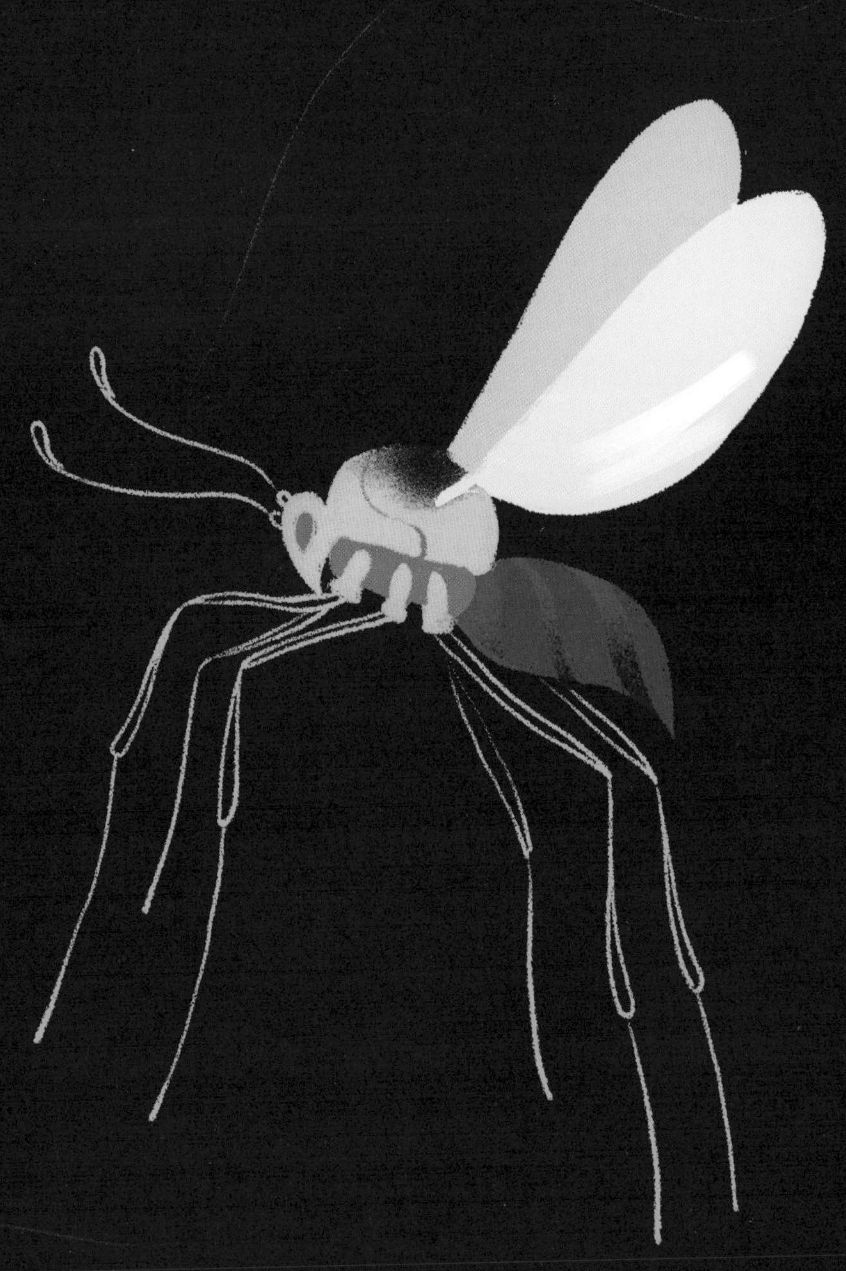

WHEN TO WORK WITH ME:

When you want to shake irritability, when you want a shift in perspective, when you want to embody your full power, when you want to feel empowered during trying times, when you want to get to the bottom of a lesson

ENERGY MEDICINE:

What is trying to get your attention? If there is an intuitive message you repeatedly ignore, it's time to heed its guidance. Otherwise you may end up in an unnecessary predicament.

If you have been feeling a bit irritated or annoyed, examine where those feeling are coming from. Let yourself get to the root of this issue.

I represent shadow work—the practice of getting to know the darker, hidden aspects of yourself. It may seem easier to turn a blind eye to traits that are potentially harmful. But taking an honest look at your darker side is the key to embodying your *full* power so that you can unconditionally love yourself.

If you are experiencing a challenging time right now, are you able to see that there may be a silver lining to what's occurring? A shift in perspective can open up endless possibility.

What is the lesson here? What is this experience trying to teach you? Keep your consciousness open so you can evolve and move forward.

POWER PRACTICE:

This power practice will give you the tools to access comfort and peace, even in times of duress. Find a place to sit comfortably and close your eyes. Imagine you are sitting outside in a field of grass. All of a sudden a swarm of gnats envelops you, surrounding your body and flitting around your head. Rather than getting annoyed and frantically swatting at them with frustration, what can you do to remain calm? How can you use your breath to stay relaxed? What mantra can you repeat to keep you present? What can you do to keep your heart open and filled with love in this moment?

As these answers present themselves, envision the gnats all moving from your body down to the warm summer grass you're seated upon, no longer a source of irritation. Write down the affirmations, breathing practices, and tools that presented so you have them handy in your spiritual tool kit to call on any time you're feeling stressed, angry, or annoyed. Thank gnat for showing you the way.

GRASSHOPPER

LEAPS OF FAITH • ROOTS • ABUNDANCE • VOICE •
MEDICINE OF SONG AND SOUND • CHANGE OF CAREER

WHEN TO WORK WITH ME:

When you want to activate more abundance in your life, when you need a dose of courage to take the leap, when you're ready to make a change in your career, when you want to confidently use your voice, when you want to bring a group together for a positive purpose

ENERGY MEDICINE:

I help activate your energy centers within so that you can take a blind leap of faith. This is the sign you've been waiting for to make a big change in your life.

I help you remember the power of your voice. What sound, song, or verbal communication needs to come from you at this time for greater healing in your life?

I can bring you healing energy, often in the form of music. I urge you to call upon your own psychic gifts and powers and know that working with a teacher or guide to do so would be helpful.

I help you align with your ancestral history and roots. Is there a family member you can call on here in the physical realm or call upon spiritually in the unseen realms to help you understand your history? Making this connection with your lineage will unlock vital wisdom within you.

I'm revered in many sacred traditions for bringing joy, prosperity, abundance, and good luck.

I remind you to be aware that your goals and desires also bring something positive to others and the world. It is important to be of service for the greater whole.

Call upon me when you need more confidence speaking your truth, when you are leading a large group, or when having a unified force is of great importance.

POWER PRACTICE:

Grasshopper has the ability to connect you with your unique soul song so you can express your truth, magic, and wisdom to the world. In this practice, you'll use breathwork to open your throat chakra (voice) so you can confidently express your personal power. Find a quiet place to sit comfortably. Begin an even breathing cycle, inhaling for 5 seconds, holding for 5 seconds, exhaling for 5 seconds, and holding for 5 seconds. As you breathe, notice the sensation of each breath and the feeling of air moving in and out of your throat as you awaken your throat chakra. Repeat this practice for a total of 2 to 3 minutes.

THE GRASSHOPPER AND SACRED TOBACCO

For members of the Abenaki tribe, indigenous to the Northeastern United States, sacred tobacco is connected to the grasshopper. Every time you pick up a grasshopper, it is said to spit out its tobacco, reminding people of its willingness to share. This is a reminder of tobacco's sacred use—an item to always share freely with others.

HAWK

SPIRITUAL REMEMBRANCE • BIGGER PICTURE • FOCUS • VISIONARY

WHEN TO WORK WITH ME:

When you are tired of dimming your inner light, when you're ready to take steps to align your life with your soul's purpose on Earth, when you need to stay focused, when you want relief, when you want to activate psychic abilities

ENERGY MEDICINE:

I am your guide for connecting you to your soul's original intention.

I help you remember why you incarnated in this life.

I am a reminder that you are ready to fly higher than ever before.

Prepare yourself for your leadership on this planet. It is time.

I am your friend in lovingly amplifying your psychic abilities, so be more observant and aware of the messages being sent to you now.

Remember, you cannot outrun your Earth mission forever. I ask you to gain a greater understanding of the powerful wisdom and abilities inside of you.

Avoid distractions. Be aware of how often you let yourself get pulled to things not truly enhancing your life. Call upon me to help you stay focused so you can most efficiently and enjoyably fulfill your life's purpose.

I am here to remind you to trust the ideas and insights that are coming to you at this time and to express them.

I am a messenger from Great Spirit.

When working with me or calling upon me to join you in your life, you will gain a heightened conscious awareness—you will have sudden flash insights, moments of clarity, and the ability to see truth more often.

POWER PRACTICE:

In this practice, you'll gain a wider perspective into your current incarnation on Earth. When hawk shows up in your life, you must look with a keen eye at what truths are revealing themselves to you. If you're working with hawk medicine, it is important to pause and view your life and relationships from a newer, wider, bigger perspective.

Get your journal and pen out. Then, close your eyes and go back in time, before you were born in this life. Envision flying up in the cosmos above our planet with an enormous hawk. Call on hawk to help you connect to the reasons you decided to incarnate on Earth in this life. Ask, "Hawk, why did I decide to incarnate in this life time? What did I come to Earth to learn? Why did I come to Earth to share my gifts and be of service?" Listen to hawk's wisdom. Then, envision climbing onto hawk's back as it flies you from the cosmos back down to your earthly body and experience. Open your eyes. Journal about what you learned during your cosmic flight with hawk.

HERON

DIGNITY • BREATH • MULTITASKING • STEPPING INTO YOUR POWER • MYSTICISM • STOICISM • CONTEMPLATION • PRECISION

WHEN TO WORK WITH ME:

When you want to access unseen realms, when you want to open to your mystic wisdom, when you want to have the fullest life experience possible, when you want to connect with your breath, when you're ready for deep contemplation

ENERGY MEDICINE:

Have you truly unlocked all the incredible wisdoms and abilities that live inside of you? I am your reminder that you have divine seer powers.

A blend of meditation and precision will give you magic. Momentary pause will provide the clear pathway for you to fly forward.

Being exposed to so many ways of life has afforded you great wisdom. If you want to expand into many more rich and deep experiences, call upon me to be your guide.

My medicines evoke the powers of breath and purification. Spiritual practices or rituals that work with these energies will benefit you at this time.

I remind you that when one door closes, another one opens. The mystic current that guides your life is truly secure and stable.

Take a moment to breathe, center yourself, and reflect on what opportunities are presenting for you right now. In this contemplation period, so much can be revealed.

POWER PRACTICE:

Heron uses a hunting strategy called "canopy feeding," where it wraps its gorgeous feathers around itself, creating what looks like an umbrella. From the shade created by this umbrella, heron is able to see and catch what it desires much more easily. For this practice, you will visualize your own canopy.

Find a quiet, dark place to sit or lie down. Close your eyes and imagine the powerful wings of heron wrapping around you, completely covering your body. This is a safe space where you are held and loved. From this place of comfort, begin an inward journey. Ask yourself, "What mystical abilities do I have within me? How can I use those abilities to step into my power? What do I want to be cleansed of before I begin this new journey?" Ask heron to use its feathers to help you achieve your desires. Sit in this canopy visualization for as long as feels right. Once the process is complete, thank heron for working with you.

HONORED THROUGHOUT HISTORY

The heron is held in high regard around the globe and throughout history. In Japan, the heron is considered to fulfill many of the requirements of Bushidō, the code of the samurai, because the bird displays a self-contained presence, carries itself with great dignity, walks with the utmost decorum, and is seldom known to exhibit any negative characteristics. In Japanese religious art, the snowy white heron is an emblem of purity and referred to as the "saintly bird." In the Druidic traditions of the ancient Celtics, the heron was regarded as a keeper of secret knowledge.

HIPPOPOTAMUS

BIRTH • REGENERATION • PROTECTION • HEALTHY EMOTIONS • WATER • SOURCE OF LIFE • DEPTH • POWERFUL • EVOCATIVE

WHEN TO WORK WITH ME:

When you're ready to deal with your emotions in a healthy way, when you want to be unaffected by other people's words, when you want to connect to parental powers and instincts, when you want to birth something new, when you want to work with the element of water

ENERGY MEDICINE:

I help you grow thicker skin so that the possible projections and words of others don't take you down.

I represent speaking the truth. My ability to open my mouth a full 180 degrees and bellow loudly reminds you to stop holding your tongue and say what needs to be said.

If you're dealing with any aggressive emotions, retreat to be alone with your energy field and spend some time in healing waters.

I remind you to trust yourself through the creative and birthing processes, whenever you're bringing something new into the world. Yes, this may require a lot from you, but you have what it takes to thrive.

Do you connect regularly with Source (the conscious energy field of all that is) or Great Spirit (Divine Creator) to find to love, light, and creativity? I open you up to receiving messages and guidance from these places, but taking the step to connect is always up to you.

As the second largest mammal on land, my medicine is strong, yet I also bring gentle healing. I honk, grunt, and groan both underwater and on land to communicate. I am your wake-up call to pay attention to your instincts.

POWER PRACTICE:

If you find yourself in a position where someone is saying mean-spirited or hurtful words about you, call on hippo to energetically protect you. Find a quiet place to sit or lie comfortably. Close your eyes and imagine yourself as a hippo standing on the banks of a river on a warm, sunny day. Feel the thick, wet layer of the hippo's skin on top of your skin, protecting you and holding you. Now, imagine that you're calmly sliding into a shallow muddy pool in the river, and begin rolling around in the mud until you're completely covered in another layer of protection. Release the negative words that were spoken. Release any energy that is not serving you. Once you feel restored, walk out of the muddy pool, lie in the sun, and allow your skin to warm as your power and truth are revived.

THE HIPPOPOTAMUS IN EGYPT

Hippos are now extinct in Egypt, but for hundreds of years, Egyptian culture revered and feared the powerful hippo, which lived alongside them on the banks of the Nile River. Ancient Egyptians looked to the hippo as symbolizing the beginning of creation; when it's submerged in water with its back visible, the hippo resembles land surrounded by water. In ancient Egyptian religion, the goddess Tauret, protector of childbirth and fertility, was represented as part hippo, part woman. This representation was likely inspired by female hippos' reputation for fiercely protecting their young.

HORSE

TRAVEL • EXPANSION • FREEDOM • PSYCHIC GIFTS • POWER • SEXUALITY • DEVOTION • LOYALTY • CONNECTION • ADVENTURE

WHEN TO WORK WITH ME:

When you want to feel free, when you want to break through limitations, when you want to unleash your full power, when you want to experience loyalty and devotion, when you are ready to embark on new adventures, when you want to have healthy sexual experiences

ENERGY MEDICINE:

I assist you in honoring and celebrating all cycles of your life, from birth to death to rebirth. Knowing that you are an infinite being allows you to access the sacredness and beauty of it all, in totality.

I am a sign that it is time to give attention, loyalty, and devotion to your most intimate relationships.

Where are you holding back in life? There is a power inside of you that wishes to be ignited and expressed. I urge you to light this power.

Sharing ideas and communication are part of my medicine. Speaking your truth with integrity and love is a vital way to be of service, so ask yourself, "How does my personal power want to be shared?"

Are you attempting to control something or someone? Remember that control is often fear-based. What fear is behind the desire to control? It's time to surrender.

I remind you that new adventures await you. Do not be afraid to set yourself free and move forward out of this constricted time with faith in these winds of change.

POWER PRACTICE:

In this practice, you're going to work with horse to help you reveal the personal power, ideas, and wisdom that you're ready to share with the world. Close your eyes, connect with your breath, and envision a beautiful green meadow. Then watch as a horse comes galloping into the middle. Observe its color, its scent, the quality of its movements. Spend a few moments simply observing and connecting with the horse. Now call the horse to you and ask it to help you answer the following question: "What true, divine power inside of me am I ready to share?" Sit with the horse as it helps you unlock your true power. Once you feel the process is complete, thank the horse for working with you. Return to your physical body and, when ready, open your eyes and journal about your experience.

HORSE IN FENG SHUI

In feng shui—the Chinese art of bringing balance and harmony to a space—a horse shown mid-gallop represents the quick arrival of one's good fortune, and feng shui experts suggest placing images of galloping horses in the living and family areas of the home.

"As the son of a cowboy, I was assigned a family horse, a magnificent gelding named Lonesome. He was strong in body and spirit, with a coal-black coat that glistened like hot tar on a railroad tie. He was not fond of cowboys or other horses and kept mostly to himself, but he loved me and I loved him.

"My father was a rodeo star, so I spent much of my childhood alone on dusty rodeo back lots, wandering about in boredom as Pop thrilled the crowds. The only company to keep was dozens of equally lonely, bored horses tied to trailers. I vetted their receptivity to my company by walking behind them, just beyond kicking distance. The horses with docile natures welcomed my presence and signaled it was safe to approach. We spent a few moments in telepathic connection as our eyes met in silent acknowledgment of our shared predicament.

"Horses were some of my first friends. They taught me a code of ethics and the art of subtle awareness. Bonding with a horse requires mutual trust and respect. To interact with a horse, one must possess the highest degree of presence and unwavering confidence. There is a dance of power between the rider and the ridden. Each must know when to yield and when to lead. As with all relationships, a balance must be achieved to sustain reciprocal benefit.

"Horses represent the paradoxical yet complementary energies of immense power and humility. They are wired for service and cooperation, and possess unparalleled physical strength, speed, and agility. They are also incredibly gentle, as if unaware of their magnitude. They've taught me to walk with grace and perseverance, to carry others when I have the strength to bear their burden, to trust with prudence and discernment, and to kick and buck when necessary."

—Luke Storey

SPIRITUAL TEACHER

HUMMINGBIRD

JOY • SWEETNESS OF LIFE • LOVE • NATURE • AWE • FLOWERS • BUILDING OR REDECORATING • INFINITY • RAINBOW

WHEN TO WORK WITH ME:

When you want to awaken more joy, when you want to be present to life's miracles, when you want to see beauty everywhere, when you want to release feelings of bitterness or resentment, when you want to have a happy home, when you need to be reminded you live in a world of infinite possibilities

ENERGY MEDICINE:

Align with me to be able to swiftly connect with joy in all situations. My flying abilities (I am the only creature who can fly backward), remind you it's possible to be lifted by experiences and memories that once felt hard. There is joy to extract from everything.

I am deeply connected with the healing power of flowers. If you want to connect with bliss, bring more flowers into your life.

I also have incredible home-building skills. Are you ready to improve, purchase, or redecorate a home? I help you create a space that serves your emotional and physical needs.

I remind you of your true nature and the realms of infinite possibilities as my wings beat extremely fast in a figure-eight pattern (the sign of infinity).

I represent love, miracles, and living a good life. If you do not want to settle, and know your worth, call upon me to help guide you to the richest experiences in life.

Reconnect now to the wonder of the present moment. Appreciate all that this Earth experience has to offer, your loved ones, and the beauty of the natural world.

POWER PRACTICE:

Hummingbird relies on flowers for nourishment. In this practice, you'll work with flowers to nourish your spirit and evoke feelings of bliss. Begin by collecting flowers from your garden, a nearby park (be sure it's OK to pick them), or your local farmer's market. Choose whatever colors, scents, and shapes call to you. Place some of the flowers, along with an image or a figurine of hummingbird, at your altar or next to your bed to reinvigorate your sacred space. Next, run a healing bath and add flower petals to the water. While you're soaking and basking in the aromatherapy of the flowers, ask jubilant hummingbird to bring your body and aura joy. Now think of six things in your life that bring you true happiness and quietly say each one as you bathe. Bask in the bliss of this moment.

THE HUMMINGBIRD IN TAINO TRADITIONS

In Taino traditions, which are rooted in present-day Caribbean islands like Cuba, the Dominican Republic, Jamaica, Haiti, Puerto Rico, and the Bahamas, the hummingbird is the symbol of the spreader of life on Earth and rebirth. The Taino believed that hummingbirds were once flies that the Sun Father (named Agueybaba) transformed into little birds. They saw the hummingbird as being very peaceful, but able to protect the homeland with the heart of an eagle. Because of this, the Taino Nation called their warriors the colibri warriors, or hummingbird warriors.

"Several years ago I experienced one of the most trying times in my adult life when my mom passed away right as I was going through a divorce and moving across the country. As soon as I started to settle into my new home, one week after my mama's death, the hummingbird began appearing as a powerful and consistent symbol of love and support, particularly in moments when I needed this reminder the most.

"In the beginning, she would often show up when I was stuck in heavy thinking, feeling sad, or calling on her for guidance. Since my mother and I sometimes had a tense relationship when she was alive, having this message in her physical absence has felt like such an especially sweet gift from her. There was a time when I was driving and crying, overwhelmed by everything imploding in my life during that first year. I had to actually slow down my car because a little green hummingbird was fluttering about right in front of my windshield and would not budge. It felt as though my mama was lovingly urging me to pause and feel the gift of peace. I went slow enough to not hit the bird and stopped at the streetlight ahead, instantly feeling a deep sense of ease and protection surrounding me.

"Another time, when my older brother and I were releasing some of her ashes during a small ceremony in the mountains near his home, we said a prayer and asked our mom to let us know that she was with us. Out of nowhere, a hummingbird rose up from behind a bush and hovered right in front of us with her wings buzzing in place. We paused in awe as my brother put his arm around me and we both drank in the moment, thanking our mama for giving us each other as we praised her life and her liberation. There are so many more auspicious and comforting moments when my mom made herself known through the sweet sounds and presence of the hummingbird. Each time this magical being appears, I experience a full-body knowing that my mama is close by and watching over me."

—Aarona Leá

AUTHOR AND COCREATOR
OF *THE MOON DECK*

JELLYFISH

LIGHT • TRANSMISSIONS • HEALTHY EMOTIONS • FLOW • MAJESTY • TUNING IN • CONTENTMENT • SILENCE • RECEIVING • HEART

WHEN TO WORK WITH ME:

When you want to feel and express your emotions in a healthy way, when you want direct access to the trust and wisdom of the Universe, when you want to connect more deeply with your heart, when you want to flow but not drift aimlessly

ENERGY MEDICINE:

I am your reminder to remain calm and go with the flow.

Are you allowing your heart intelligence to guide your way? Communicate with your heart and flow from there.

Tune in to what your emotions are teaching you at this time and let yourself be lifted by the love and realizations. A majestic exploration of your emotional depths will serve you.

Work with the wind. I rely on this element to take me where I need to go in life. I can help you access its guidance.

When moving toward your goal, have a plan in mind. This ensures you're in flow but not drifting aimlessly and wasting time.

I represent clear consciousness energies. Work with me to allow your complete faith in the Universe to take hold.

POWER PRACTICE:

In this meditation exercise, you'll practice stillness and going with the flow, two powerful properties of jellyfish. Find a quiet place to sit, and call upon jellyfish to work with you. Close your eyes and begin to imagine yourself as a jellyfish floating in water. What shape and colors are you? What do your tentacles look like? How does light shine through your transparent body? How does the water and wind feel on your skin as you float along? Once you've imagined yourself as a jellyfish, sit still for 5 minutes. Do nothing, just breathe. This practice of stillness will strengthen your ability to remain calm and trust in all that is.

ANCIENT AND REMARKABLE

Jellyfish are some of the oldest organisms on Earth; fossil records show that they even predate the evolution of teeth, claws, and bone and have been around for at least half a billion years. One particular type of jellyfish, called a hydrozoan, has the profound ability to actually revert back to a polyp, an organism's first stage of existence.

KANGAROO

WORKING IN TANDEM WITH MOTHER EARTH • MOVING FORWARD • STAMINA • PROTECTION OF THE VULNERABLE

WHEN TO WORK WITH ME:

When you want to move forward, when you want stability and balance in your life, when you want to honor Great Mother Earth, when you want to show true kindness toward children and animals, when you want to eliminate or move past distractions

ENERGY MEDICINE:

There is no time for nonsense. Take an honest look at the unhealthy distractions in your life and move past them. It's time to shift from a small, narrow view to a higher perspective and make the jump.

I help you move in a bold way, working from your gut feelings and intuition.

Do not look or move backward. I urge you to focus on what is ahead of you and take powerful steps in that direction.

If you are struggling with procrastination, call upon me now to help you take a powerful leap in the right direction. My medicine will push you forward in life.

Are there children or vulnerable creatures whom you can spend more time giving love, protection, and support to? I am known for protecting small beings with a powerful maternal instinct. Ask yourself whether you can help a fellow creature in need at this time.

I remind you of the importance of being grounded and connected to Great Mother Earth. You'll move forward best when you feel centered and strong in your body.

POWER PRACTICE:

Find a quiet place where you can stand barefoot comfortably, ideally outside. Once there, call upon kangaroo to join you in this ritual and to empower you with its medicine. Get clear on one aspect of your life that you are ready to leave behind. This can be a personal behavior, pattern, limiting belief, relationship, job, and so on. Envision that aspect as a word or words surrounding your feet in a circle. Thank this aspect for its teachings and tell it out loud, "With honor and gratitude, I now release you." Then, think of a word you'd like to experience—something new, bold, or optimistic. Envision that word in a new circle on the ground that you will jump to. Then, when you are ready, say, "I now choose ___ (say the word you envision in the circle)," envision yourself as a powerful kangaroo, and jump to the new word. Once there, take a few moments to close your eyes and really see, feel, taste, smell, and hear yourself already living this new experience. Allow it to come alive. Once you feel fully integrated, express to kangaroo, Great Mother Earth, and Great Spirit that you are ready for their blessings and guidance to achieve this goal, and ask that they show you the way.

LONG JUMPERS

Kangaroos are excellent inspiration for forward motion, as they cannot move backward on land. These long-distance jumpers can clear over 15 feet [4.5 m] in one hop and move as fast as 30 miles [48 km] per hour, aided by their strong legs and tail, which is used as a fifth limb when moving and for balance when hopping.

KIWI

BIRTHING GRAND IDEAS • SPIRITUAL AWARENESS • DISCERNMENT • SENSE OF SMELL • GIVING AND RECEIVING • EARTH GUARDIAN • UNITY • THE MOON

WHEN TO WORK WITH ME:

When you want to discern honesty from dishonesty, when you want to work more deeply with Earth medicine, when you want more sweetness in your life, when you want to bring people and causes together, when you want to spend more time in the forest

ENERGY MEDICINE:

Call upon me to enhance your powerful ability to tell what is honest and true.

I am a flightless bird. I stay closely connected to Great Mother Earth, and her medicine and guidance. I empower your connection to your body and the Earth plane, both imperative aspects for embodying your full power. If you want to learn how to manifest your Earthly goals, work with me.

My medicine helps nourish you at night and during any moon ceremonies.

I elevate kindness, love, humility, and sweetness in your life.

I represent unity medicine. I serve as a bridge to unite worlds. Call upon me to create community and bring together family.

I work with the powers of the forest. If you're looking to immerse yourself in these environments, you can call on me for protection and positive experiences.

POWER PRACTICE:

In this practice, we'll work with nocturnal energy and kiwi. At the next new and full moons, find a place where you can be safely outside at night—a backyard, a public beach, etc.—and find a quiet, comfortable place where you can lie on your back directly on the ground. Call upon kiwi to work with you in opening your connection to Great Mother Earth. Close your eyes and imagine kiwi next to you. See its small brown body and narrow beak. Ask kiwi how you can work with Great Mother Earth to restore and enhance your full power. What experiences or activities will connect you to the Earth's magic? Call upon kiwi to fortify you and assist you in these endeavors.

THE KIWI IN MĀORI TRADITION

The kiwi, a flightless bird native to New Zealand, comes out mostly at night. In Māori tradition, it is known as te manu huna a Tāne, "the hidden bird of Tāne" (god of the forest). In this same tradition, kiwi feathers are woven into kahu kiwi, rare, beautiful cloaks worn for sacred ceremonial occasions. During my participation in an ancient Māori practice with three Māori elders, I reconnected to my past lives. One elder who wore a kahu kiwi recognized the experience I was having, and during our conversation, a feather lifted off his cloak and drifted to me. I knew this was a sign from Great Spirit and the power animal world recognizing my path and truth.

The humble flightless kiwi, humble yet strong.

Native icon of Aotearoa, New Zealand.

Known by many local and visitors from afar, hence the household name.

Comes out at night to search for food, grubs, and tasty insects . . .

The mating call of the male kiwi is a quiet sound.

The mating call of the female is a loud screech.

The legs of the kiwi are solid and extremely dangerous when protecting itself and its burrow underground.

Very rarely can the kiwi be seen in broad daylight.

It is under the cover of night that it comes out to feed.

—Matua Ruia Kereopa
(Te Kouorehua)
MĀORI ELDER

KOALA

REST AND RELAXATION • CALMNESS • STEADY CLIMB • MYSTICAL KNOWINGNESS • WONDER • SHARING LOVE • FORGIVENESS • RELEASE

WHEN TO WORK WITH ME:

When you want to slow down and relax, when you want to release anger, when you want to open up paternal instincts, when you want to be less reactive, when you want to release addiction to drama or stress, when you want to forgive, when you want to let go of grudges and animosity, when you want to experience awe, when you want to trust the big picture

ENERGY MEDICINE:

My medicine helps you release grudges and find the ability to forgive. Is there anyone (yourself included) you could send forgiveness to? This can be done energetically, or through personal communication.

Call upon me when you need to be less reactive and more centered. I empower an even-keel state of emotions, allowing you to operate with heart-centered clarity rather than reacting from a place of ego and defensiveness.

I am your reminder that it's time to rest and go with the flow. If you have been pushing too hard or leaning into drama, anxiety, or stress, consider whether you have become addicted to this way of being. Do you trust things can be different?

I'm here to help you remember your true divine nature. Aside from all that's going on externally, what are the ancient truths that live inside of you?

I represent Great Mother Earth nourishment, the womb, and parental love. Is there any healing work that you could do to tend to your inner child or your relationship with parents or children?

POWER PRACTICE:

Koalas are associated with the element of clay, and with unwinding and relaxation. For this practice you will need a healing clay, like bentonite clay, to apply to your face and body.

Standing in front of the mirror in your bathroom, call upon koala to work with you in releasing what is no longer serving you. Ask koala to be with you as you relax and restore love to your being.

Now, set an intention for what you are going to release today—it could be an emotion, a relationship, stress, or anxiety. With love and care, slowly spread the wet clay on your face or whatever part of your body you wish to cover. Once you've finished, give yourself at least 20 minutes to let the clay dry. As the clay dries and tightens, imagine it is drawing out the things you are ready to release.

Let your intuition and spirit guide you during the drying process. You can sit or lie down in meditation, or go outside and sit on the ground to connect with the Earth. Maybe you feel inclined to talk to koala about the things you're releasing to understand how they were trying to protect you or teach you. Or maybe you feel like being completely present and still, honoring the process you are completing.

Once the clay is dry, return to your bathroom and wash the clay away in the sink or shower. Feel the water cleanse, clear, and purify you. Watch as what you've released runs down the drain in the form of clay.

To close this purifying ritual, apply some nourishing cream or coconut oil to the area the clay covered. As you spread the cream on your body, send yourself healing and uplifting energies. You now have space for them. Thank koala for helping you release the things you no longer needed to carry.

KOI

EASE AND GRACE • DEEPER CONSCIOUSNESS • ZEN • PASSION • MEDITATION • HONORING ANCESTORS • PROSPERITY • HEALTHY FRIENDSHIPS

WHEN TO WORK WITH ME:

When you need more peace and calm, when you want to have a stronger meditative practice, when you want to connect with your ancestors, when you want to appreciate or invite in meaningful friendships, when you want financial success and wealth

ENERGY MEDICINE:

I bring Zen energy and remind you that having more peace and calm in your life is essential. Do not fool yourself into believing that chaos and struggle have to be the norm.

By making gratitude and meditation an integral part of each day, you will experience much more harmony, fulfillment, and ease in your life.

If you are ready to create a deeper connection with the wisdom of your ancestors, call upon me to assist.

Could any of your friendships benefit from you opening your heart and acting with compassion? Don't let your ego get in the way of true connection.

Wealth and prosperity are two of my main medicines. Call upon me to teach you how to seize the opportunities that will bring forth abundance.

If you are in a transformative phase and truly believe in the new direction you want to go, I activate the ability to keep swimming, even when the current is against you.

POWER PRACTICE:

In this practice, you'll work with koi's ability to reveal the areas in your life that need your attention. Begin by sitting or lying with your eyes closed. Picture yourself walking up to a massive koi pond where the biggest koi you've ever seen are harmoniously gliding through the water. As you stand at the water's edge, mesmerized by their beauty, imagine entering the pond as a koi. Choose your koi color: gold, orange, or red. Only proceed to the next part of the practice once you've become clear on what color you are.

- If you are a gold koi, swim in the waters while calling upon more financial wealth and prosperity to be bestowed upon you. What baggage, emotional blocks, or fears are standing in the way of success?

- If you are an orange koi, express gratitude for the friendships in your life as you swim. Consider whether there are relationships where you could be kinder or more compassionate and attentive.

- If you are a red koi, focus on love and passion as you move through the water. Consider what areas of your life you currently feel the most passion about and what you can do to infuse the rest of your life with that level of passion.

When you are complete, thank koi for the realizations that emerged in the waters.

FROM FISH TO DRAGON

In Chinese culture, the koi is known to represent good fortune, strength, and perseverance. One ancient Chinese legend tells the story of a determined koi that swam upstream to the base of a waterfall on the Yellow River. Though the rest of the fish in its school gave up, this koi continued to jump until it reached the top of the falls. The gods rewarded the koi by turning it into a golden dragon.

"During a Vipassana silent retreat, I often sat by the pond in the compound. I was told there were fish in the pond, but I never saw any. One day, I was walking down the path to the pond and heard the voice of my deceased ssenga ('auntie' in my father's tongue of Luganda). She had passed away a few months prior to the retreat. She said to me clearly, 'Come closer to the water; I am coming to you.' It was the first time since she had transitioned that she called out to me.

"As I neared the water's edge, I saw a beautiful golden koi swim out from beneath the leaves. It swam right up to me and stopped. I could hear my ssenga saying, 'All is well; I am fine. I am traveling and I am with you. Continue to root deeper into your Bone Healing medicine, for the ancestors are with you *now*.'

"This was a profound experience because although I work with power animals in my practice, the koi was not an animal that had ever come to assist me. I've always understood, though, that Spirit and the ancestors speak to me in myriad ways.

"Since then, I work with the koi often when I am moved to speak to my ssenga or work with my ancestors' energy in consciously awakening feelings of prosperity, abundance, and growth. Now, my visions of what is to come into abundance are so much stronger. I can channel the energies of the koi simply by visualizing the koi swimming in the pond where I first made her acquaintance and received and embodied her magical energy. I call out the word *kwagala* ('love' in Luganda) and she appears. I receive knowledge, wisdom, and answers to questions regarding myself and other people, both alive and those who have transitioned.

"The koi provides us with the knowledge that there is a rebirth upon us; that abundance and prosperity are our birthright; that it is time to deepen our connections with our higher self. I use the following affirmation 'I am loved and supported, I commit to expressing my higher self, I am.'"

—Ssanyu Birigwa

INDIGENOUS BONE HEALER SHAMAN, M.S. IN NARRATIVE MEDICINE, AND ADJUNCT PROFESSOR AT COLUMBIA UNIVERSITY

KOMODO DRAGON

BRUTE STRENGTH • ACTION • QUICK AND DECISIVE • NEWFOUND POWER • INITIATION • DETOXIFICATION

WHEN TO WORK WITH ME:

When you need to be stronger than ever before, when you want to summon a powerful new energy within you, when you need to take swift and decisive action, when you need to stand strong in the face of other people's opinions, when you need to step boldly into a new life, when you need to exit a toxic situation

ENERGY MEDICINE:

My energy is powerful. I carry a massive new life force, delivering energy that brings radical awakening or creative revelation. Both are meant to snap you out of your current situation and help you move on to bigger and better things.

As new energy comes alive within you, it is vital that you are as clear and heart-centered as possible. All that you do right now has amplified power and carries strong ripple effects.

If you are clear on what you need and want at this time, stay grounded and resolute. Do not allow anyone or anything undermine your endeavors or intuition.

If your environment is unhealthy in any way, I remind you that rather than further engaging, it might be better to walk away.

If you are standing at what feels like an important crossroads in life, this is an initiation for you, a miraculous opportunity to shed an old way of living and boldly step forward into a new way of being.

POWER PRACTICE:

This practice will help you clear toxicity or dysfunction in your life. Get a pen and a piece of paper or a journal, and call forward mighty Komodo dragon to work with you by saying, "Sacred Komodo power animal, join me now in this sacred process." Now draw two columns on the paper. Label the left column "Toxic" and the right column "Healthy." With the fierce medicine of Komodo dragon by your side, begin to list anything that feels even remotely dysfunctional or unhealthy in the left column. It can be people, behaviors, habits, foods, and so on. Whatever comes up, let it out. Once that is complete, move to the right column, and with the loving power of Komodo, list the things in your life that are healthy and bring you love, joy, high vibrations, healing, happiness, and abundance.

Once that is complete, return to the left column and circle two things from the "Toxic" list that you will commit to eradicating from your life. Ask Komodo dragon for support as you spend some time sitting with what it will mean to clear these aspects. Now look at the list on the right. How can these things support and encourage you as you eliminate toxicity? It is only when we bravely confront what is not serving us—the relationships, behaviors, and stories that keep us from thriving—that we can attain true liberation. Return to this exercise whenever you feel toxic or dysfunctional energy taking up space in your life.

STRENGTH, POWER, AND SMELL

Embodying its spiritual teachings of brute strength and power, the Komodo dragon is the largest lizard in the world, measuring up to 10 feet [3 m] long. Evoking its power-animal medicine of sensing what is not healthy and thriving, a Komodo dragon can sense a dead animal from over 5 miles [8 km] away and determine the exact location by "smelling" the air using its flickering tongue.

LADYBUG

RELEASING WORRY • DIVINE PROTECTION • BLESSINGS • GOOD FORTUNE • FLOW • HIGHER CONSCIOUSNESS

WHEN TO WORK WITH ME:

When you want to experience more joy and good fortune, when you need energetic protection, when you want to activate higher consciousness, when you want to connect to the power of the present moment

ENERGY MEDICINE:

I am here to remind you that life is a fleeting, miraculous experience. Remember to keep things in perspective and to pick your battles, knowing your time here in this earthly existence is precious.

Are you allowing yourself to be pulled out of the present moment too often? Be more consciously aware of tendencies to drift into past or future thoughts. When that happens, lovingly bring your focused attention to the centerline of your being and breathe into the present. All we have is this moment.

Call upon me any time you are entering into a situation, place, conversation, or business deal where you need an extra layer of divine protection to empower you.

I bring messages of the New Paradigm—the time on Earth where old ways, systems, patterns, and behaviors that created separation, division, and fear fall away in order for the new, higher-consciousness energies to amplify and take hold. When you want the New Paradigm to activate within you, call upon my energy medicine.

I bring an extra abundance of joy into your life. If you are feeling slightly "off," or experiencing the blues, call upon me to remind your cells, soul, and being that joy is your birthright.

POWER PRACTICE:

In this practice, you will call on ladybug to bless the path ahead. Sit or stand in a comfortable position, with your palms together at your chest. Ask ladybug to join you in activating new, positive energy. Begin rubbing your hands together in front of your heart to activate a new energy field. Ask your soul what feeling would serve it most at this time—joy, creativity, healing, love, passion, or whatever else calls to you. Whatever your word is, see and feel it being activated by the rubbing of your hands, coming alive, and filling your aura, the energetic space surrounding your body. Now begin to move your hands around your body, continuing to rub them together, clearing any areas that feel stuck or stagnated.

When you have finished moving your hands around your body, invite ladybug to bless this new energy. Now clap your hands together to activate this new emotion within your physical body. End by repeating the following phrase five times: "I am here, and in this moment, I am the most powerful love imaginable. I am centered, clear, and thriving. And so it is."

LADYBUGS AND THE VIRGIN MARY

Ladybugs have long been associated with providing divine protection and releasing worry. One legend dating back to the Middle Ages tells of crops all across Europe being destroyed by insect pests. The desperate farmers prayed for help from the Virgin Mary, and as the story goes, soon after, swarms of red bugs showed up, saving the crops by preying on the harmful pests. In thanks to the Virgin Mary, the farmers named the bugs "the beetles of Our Lady," which later evolved to "lady beetles," and finally, "ladybugs," as we call them in the United States. Some historians also speculate that the ladybug's red wings were associated with the red coat Mary wears in medieval artwork.

LEECH

DETOXIFICATION • REVERENCE FOR NATURE • LINEAGE HEALING • HIDDEN VALUE • ALCHEMY • NEW LIFE FORCE

WHEN TO WORK WITH ME:

When you want to feel reinvigorated and strong, when you want to release judgments or fears, when you want to remove toxicity, when you want your life to head in a new direction, when you want more trust, when you're going through a big transition

ENERGY MEDICINE:

Call upon me to work with you to help you face your fears in order to transmute and transcend them. This act of alchemy will shift fear to love.

I help you remember that big changes in life don't need to be painful, and that patience and trust are your greatest allies.

One of my main medicines is conjuring new life force. If you are ready to heal on a mind, body, spirit, or soul level, call upon me to extract toxins and stimulate a new circulation of energy.

I remind you that snap judgments can prevent connection and progress. Are you jumping too quickly to conclusions? Is there a person or an idea that you could get to know better before deciding it's not for you? I encourage you to keep an open mind and an open heart.

What negative pattern, belief, habit, or mindset are you ready to face and release? Call upon me to show you the way.

I remind you of the power and miracles of the unseen realms. If you have called upon divine support, then trust the spiritual path to guide your way.

POWER PRACTICE:

In this practice, you'll work with leech to extract fear-based energy. Sit comfortably, close your eyes, and connect with your breath, inhaling each breath into your heart center, the space in the middle of your chest. Call upon sacred leech to work with you in this meditation, and allow brave self-inquiry as you ask your heart, "What fear am I finally ready to release so I can experience a better life?" Keep asking your heart this question until an answer is revealed. Where does this fear manifest for you? Are you holding it in your chest, your stomach, your back? Once you've located the fear, ask leech to go to that place on your body. Imagine a leech gently attaching to you and extracting this fearful, toxic energy. Stay with this process until the leech has removed all it needs to, then feel it detach from your body. Now send deep, loving breaths to that area, feeling it relax and warm as it floods with love. Thank leech and ask it to return to you when you need to transform fear into love.

"During one of my healing adventures in life, I medicinal ceremony. I worked with a renowned leech therapy above my liver for detoxification level of nervousness, viewing leeches as slimy them work their healing powers, my viewpoint complete reverence. These creatures are astoun-selves to be open-minded, we can transmute

was called to work with leeches in a sacred,
leech therapist from Austria, who conducted
and cleansing. I began the process with a high
or scary. But during my time with them, feeling
almost instantaneously shifted to one of
ding. They remind us that when we allow our-
fear to love."

—Alyson Charles

LEOPARD

EMBRACING YOUR UNIQUENESS • KNOWING YOUR POWER • ACTIVATING CONFIDENCE • LEADERSHIP • INDEPENDENCE • INTELLIGENCE • PERSISTENCE

WHEN TO WORK WITH ME:

When you're ready to embrace what makes you unique, when you want to deepen your spiritual gifts, when you need to build self-confidence, when you're ready to release ego, when you're stepping into a leadership role

ENERGY MEDICINE:

I remind you to connect with your soul's truth and your unique, personal medicine. What are your unique "spots"? Embrace them and show them to the world.

I help you release hypercritical or judgmental thoughts about yourself and others so that you can move into a softer and more compassionate energetic space.

I represent leadership without ego. Guide and empower others from your heart space and soul wisdom, knowing we are all mirrors and teachers for one another.

I embody true confidence. Call on my leopard medicine to activate within you when you need to act with self-assuredness and poise.

I know how to harness and employ my strong energy, and I can help you learn how to use your own energy responsibly. Consider what energy you bring into a room or situation and understand the profound power you have to shift a dynamic.

My aura emanates elegance, luxury, and power. Call upon me to strengthen these qualities in you too.

Independence, intelligence, and persistence are three medicine traits I empower in you. I remind you to stand for yourself and be proud of who you are, but to do it all with a regal, humble nature and grace.

POWER PRACTICE:

This practice is inspired by leopard's aura—a luminous radiating energy field. Auras are often associated with colors, which can change over time. In many spiritual traditions, aura reading, clearing, and healing are common practices, and knowing the state of your auric field can help you feel clearer and brighter.

You'll need a partner for this exercise. Stand directly in front of a white wall and have your partner stand 8 to 9 feet [2.4 to 2.7 m] away. Begin by having them gaze at your third eye (the center of your forehead) for at least 30 seconds, then have them slowly move their gaze to trace the edges of your body. Ask them to tell you what color or colors are revealed as they scan, then read about the significance of each color below:

- Red may mean you're expressing or feeling passion and are grounded and connected to the Earth and your body.
- Orange may mean your creative energies are really flowing and that you're in a powerful time of regeneration.
- Yellow may mean that your authentic light and power are expressing and that joyful radiance is emanating.
- Green may mean that your heart is healing, or that you're exuding compassion, unconditional love, and forgiveness.
- Blue may mean that you need to communicate or have been communicating something important, or that you're experiencing a sense of peace, and tranquility.
- Purple may mean that your spiritual gifts are opening, that your intuition and connection to spirit guides and unseen realms are alive, and that you're tapped into your divine truth.

LION

COMMANDING • SUPREME RULER • GENEROSITY • COURAGE • DIGNITY • ENTHUSIASM • NEW FRIENDSHIP • HONESTY

WHEN TO WORK WITH ME:

When you want to act from a place of honesty and integrity, when you need more courage, when you want to be a respected leader, when you're ready to approach life with vigor and passion, when you want healthy new friendships, when you want to be more generous

ENERGY MEDICINE:

My strong energy gives you the power to trust in yourself and your abilities. If you are in a period of life where you're being tested or initiated, remember you have *all* that you need within to rise to the moment and overcome whatever is thrown your way.

I am a natural born leader. Call upon me to empower you and provide confidence when you're ready to lead or take charge.

If you have been experiencing jealousy or envy, work with me to clear these negative energies and provide clarity so that you can be more compassionate toward yourself.

Generosity is one of my main medicines. Think now of whom you can better support. How can you help others in attaining their dreams? What assistance can you offer?

My powerful roar and posture reminds you to protect those you love.

Can honesty have a bigger place in your life? Is there something you need to come clean about, or is there someone else you feel could be more forthright? Work with me to embody the courage needed to activate more honesty and clear the air.

POWER PRACTICE:

To bring lion medicine into your life, you will focus on connecting with your heart energy. Take a moment to meditate on the illustration here of lion and, while doing so, ask yourself at least three times (pausing between each to let the answers reveal themselves), "What does it mean to have the heart of a lion?" Write the answers on a piece of paper or in your journal. Keep your reflections on your bedside table, and for the next week read through these words before you go to bed and first thing when you wake up in the morning. Call forward these qualities into your heart. Invite lion's supreme medicine into your life and consider what actions you can take to cultivate a lion's heart.

A SYMBOL OF COURAGE AND VALOR

The lion is often associated with nobility, royalty, and supreme power and has appeared as a symbol in many ancient spiritual and cultural traditions for thousands of years. In medieval times, lions were used on crests in times of war to represent courage, bravery, and royalty. These crests were found in Denmark, Finland, Jerusalem, Spain, Ireland, the Netherlands, among others. In Egyptian mythology, Sekhmet, the fierce goddess of war, sun, and fire, was depicted with the head of a lioness and the body of a woman. Hot desert winds were associated with her fiery breath.

LIZARD

DREAMS • TRANSFORMATION • ADAPTATION • SUNSHINE • HEALTHY BOUNDARIES • INTERNAL POWER • GRATITUDE

WHEN TO WORK WITH ME:

When you are ready to initiate change in your life, when you are ready to let go of what you've clung to in the past, when you want to transcend fear, when you need support moving forward, when you want to understand and act upon messages in your dreams

ENERGY MEDICINE:

Are you ready for change? I initiate powerful (and sometimes immediate) transformation and help you become more adaptable. Call upon me when you want strength in living a new way.

I am symbolic of great inner power. I represent being able to regenerate after letting go of what I know I must in order to truly live.

I remind you to pay close attention to your dreams. What are they revealing?

I help you set healthy boundaries and detach from situations or people when necessary so you can be happier and more fulfilled.

Are you gripping too tightly to control? I can align you with flow and surrender if you ask for my help.

I am very sensitive to vibration. If I am resonating with you, working with healing sounds, tuning forks, and chanting will enhance your life.

I align with the medicine of the sun. Access my energy by spending time soaking up the great solar rays of Earth's closest star.

POWER PRACTICE:

In this practice, you'll call on lizard to help you unveil the hidden messages in your dreams. Keep a dream journal and a pen beside your bed. When you get in bed at night, close your eyes and visualize a lizard as you drift off. Let your mind follow the lizard wherever it wants to go—maybe it's basking in the sun, or crawling across rocks, or darting up a tree. Let this image gently disappear as you slip into sacred rest. If you wake up in the night, write down any visions or experiences you've had in your dreams before you go back to sleep—it's important to capture them before they fade away. Then devote some time each week or month to read through your entries and connect with what was revealed during dreamtime. What fears, hopes, or messages are arising? Are any themes or patterns emerging? Call on lizard to help you access the knowledge your subconscious wants to reveal to you.

SHEDDING FOR SURVIVAL

In true representation of their medicine of immediate transformation and adaptation, some lizards have the amazing ability to shed their tails when they are caught by predators. The tail, which continues to move for a short while after being detached, distracts the predator and gives the lizard a chance to escape.

"I was living in Costa Rica in my early twenties, during what turned out to be one of the most transformative times of my life. Every morning when I woke up, this iguana was always in my living room, and I developed a friendship with him. I named him Donut and fed him chopped greens, which he loved.

"Fast-forward more than a decade later, when I purchased my first animal card deck. I kept pulling the iguana. I was baffled and, for some reason, resistant to the fact that a little reptile was one of my animal guides. I remembered my experience with Donut and began to dig deeper. I read about the meanings (strength, gratitude, transformation, and awareness). I always observed Donut, and he exuded those characteristics in his way.

"Iguanas are strong and very aware, sensitive creatures. I began to connect with the iguana totem through meditation and prayer. In August of last year, during a plant medicine ceremony, I was deep in meditation. I had such a vivid vision of two iguanas climbing onto my knees, looking right at me, then turning into white light, which went right up to my third eye, then to my crown. I had come to that ceremony with a firm intention of helping transmute a difficult time in my life, and I felt the message of transformation and the effects of it from that experience.

"The iguana continues to be one of the few animal guides I turn to when I need strength during a time of transformation. The iguana has also popped up many more times in such interesting ways through energetic readings, dreams, and random conversations. It's always a reminder that we are in alignment, and our guides are watching over us."

—Sanjay
MUSICIAN

LLAMA

INTEGRATION • SPIRITUAL CALLING • WHOLENESS • TRUSTWORTHINESS • SUPPORT • SERENITY • CALMNESS • FUN

WHEN TO WORK WITH ME:

When you want to feel a sense of connection, when you want to experience serenity, when you want to express yourself truthfully, when you want support, when you need more fun in your life, when you want your business or career to be infused with spirituality

ENERGY MEDICINE:

When life is feeling heavy and serious, I bring you medicine of joy and fun, reminding you that sometimes the best way to feel centered and powerful is to make time for laughter and play.

Any time you're cutting off aspects of yourself from being freely expressed, work with me to bring you back into authentic alignment.

I live in the present moment and embody deep calm and serenity. I remind you to be unbothered. Envision an energy shield around you and do not let anyone or anything pull you out of your peace and power.

Remember, you are not too broken, and you are not too wounded, to live your grandest dreams. You are already whole and beautiful, and you simply need to reconnect back to your personal power.

I assist you in bringing spirituality to every aspect of your life, including your career. Division does not serve you, and I help unite your worlds.

I am at peace because I am aware of my connection to the entire web of life. I remind you to be mesmerized by the miracles of your existence.

POWER PRACTICE:

In this exercise, you will practice being unbothered by tapping into llama's calm energy. Sit or stand comfortably and close your eyes. Envision yourself as a llama steadily and happily walking on a trail through the mountains, breathing in the fresh air, feeling the breeze and sunshine. Next, envision a rainbow appearing above you, arching over your path and moving with you as you make your way forward. This energetic shield empowers you to not let anyone or anything pull you out of your peace and power. If you notice any sense of agitation or restlessness, tune back in to the colors and power of the rainbow field and see the agitation leaving completely. Connect to your breath and the rainbow as much as you need. You can call on this practice whenever you need to tap into a moment of calm—at home, at work.

THE LLAMA IN INCAN CULTURE

Llamas were first domesticated by the Incas over 3,000 years ago. The Incas used the animals' soft wool for weaving, and their relatively easy-going nature made them easy to socialize and train as pack animals. Llamas were sometimes buried with nobility, indicating their significance in Incan culture.

MACAW

INNOVATION • SACRED UNION • EXTROVERSION • CEREMONY • THE SUN • REGENERATION OF LIFE • SONG • ENHANCED MOOD • COLOR

WHEN TO WORK WITH ME:

When you want to use the power of your voice, when you're ready to meet your sacred partner, when you want to connect with the power of the sun, when you want to bring positive energy to the world, when you want to be more extroverted, when you're done feeling like you're "too much," when you want to proudly express your uniqueness

ENERGY MEDICINE:

I remind you to take energetic responsibility. Your energy may be so strong that it dictates the energy of the room, so be sure to be aware of what you're bringing into each situation.

I represent fresh ideas and innovation. If a new path is presenting itself for your life, ask your heart chakra whether it feels like a positive move, and if the answer is yes, then go for it.

Do you want to find your voice or enhance your singing abilities? Call upon me to work with you during dreamtime to show you how to express yourself through sound.

If your life has been feeling dull, think about what activities and gifts you have that add colorful vibrancy to your experiences. You hold the power to brighten your life. What can you do today to lift your spirit?

I embody healthy and committed pair bonding, so call upon me to assist in finding sacred partnership filled with fidelity and honor.

I represent extrovert energy and confidence. Allow me to release feelings of shyness so you can speak and listen with presence and radiance.

POWER PRACTICE:

Macaw represents expressing your unique song and colors unapologetically. To tap into macaw's bold energy, stand in front of a mirror and call this sacred bird forward. Close your eyes and envision yourself soaring through a rainforest as a macaw. See your bright, colorful wings flapping and hear your powerful voice ringing through the trees. Make your presence known. Fly for as long as you'd like. When the flight is complete, land on a branch and then return to your physical body. Open your eyes, and as you gaze into your own eyes in the mirror, say, "My unique voice, power, and song are needed here on Earth. I am never 'too much.' I allow myself to freely and beautifully *be me*." Repeat this as many times as needed. When done, thank macaw for being with you and invite it to continue to work with you in bringing forward your unique offerings here on Earth.

A VOCAL BIRD

True to their bold, extroverted energy, macaws vocalize for 5 to 10 minutes several times a day and are so loud that they can be heard from as far as 5 miles [8 km] away.

SYMBOL OF SACRED UNION

The Bororo tribe of Brazil considers the macaw to be a messenger of the gods and ancestors, and a symbol of sacred union. This is rooted in the fact that macaws mate for life.

"When my family and I escaped Iran, we settled in California and my mother adopted a macaw, which she named Paco.

"My mom brought Paco with us on road trips. Once, when I was a teen, I spent a long night on magic mushrooms. The next day, I was sitting in our VW van and suddenly, I could hear Paco speak. Maybe it was the mushrooms or maybe it was the intimacy of sharing a van seat with him, but for the first time, I really saw Paco—his beautiful green and blue feathers, the dark outline of his eyes, and the strong beak that could break your finger. We gazed at each other, and he told me about his life; how, as a baby, he'd been abducted by poachers from a lush garden in the Amazon; smuggled and almost suffocated in a carry-on bag on a plane to Miami; then, shoved in a hot cage with hundreds of other macaws on a long truck drive to California, where those that survived would become someone's pet. We communicated with a telepathic talent neither of us knew we had.

"As we spoke, I decided I'd set Paco free. I knew life in captivity meant he might have lost his survival skills, but I'd seen macaws in Los Angeles who'd escaped pet stores and created colonies. I hoped Paco could find other macaws to teach him to fly from palm tree to oak tree, eat orchard fruit, and caw with abandonment. Though Paco's life in the wild might be short, I figured it would be better than spending his days driving in a hot van with cranky teens.

"We arrived at a beach parking lot and while my mom unloaded the car, I stealthily opened Paco's cage, then walked toward the ocean. Suddenly, I heard my mom yelling that Paco had gotten loose. He landed on a telephone pole, then tested his wings, which hadn't been trimmed recently. Soon, he found some leverage and flew away. We never saw Paco again.

"Years later, I was sitting with my daughter under a big oak and I heard cawing. I looked up and could swear I saw Paco looking directly at me. We locked eyes for a moment, and then, he took off. At the time, I was asking the universe if I should pursue my passion in theater. I was looking for an answer, and I felt like seeing Paco, free to fly, was a sign for me to say yes to life and all its possibilities."

—Shiva Rose

AUTHOR OF *WHOLE BEAUTY*, ALCHEMIST, AND FOUNDER OF THE WELLNESS WEBSITE, THE LOCAL ROSE

MANATEE

ANCIENT WATER WISDOM • SWEET LOVE • HEALING • SOOTHED HEART • GENTLENESS • TRUST • INTUITION

WHEN TO WORK WITH ME:

When your heart needs healing, when you want to be more trusting of yourself and others, when you want to evoke ancient wisdom, when you want to awaken your intuition, when you want to experience gentle love and soothing peace

ENERGY MEDICINE:

My connections to ancient beings and water bring you the ability to spiritually awaken with grace and ease.

You do not need to rush. You will be best served by pausing to feel energetically what next step will uplift and empower you.

I call you to be soft and gentle, not forceful or violent. Moving forward with a gentle, open heart combined with spiritual healing is always better than operating with force.

I'm here to remind you that your sensitivities and empathy are spiritual gifts. Allow those around you to have their experiences while you remain in your energy, awareness, and power.

Remember that even if your heart has been hurt in the past, you can learn to trust yourself and others again. Call upon me to soothe your heart and bring clarity to the situation so that you can let go of any baggage.

I am often most comfortable by myself or with a sacred partner. Big groups are not for me, and it's OK if it's the same for you.

POWER PRACTICE:

If you've gone through a painful breakup or a difficult relationship, beautiful manatee can soothe your heart and help you learn to trust in love again. To connect with manatee energy, set time aside for a healing bath. Before the bath, call for manatee's gentle, kind ways to be with you. Tune in to your heart to decide what should go in the bathwater, picking things that are soothing and uplifting. Perhaps it's drops of your favorite essential oils, petals of your favorite flower, Epsom salts, or crystals (be sure they are safe to use in water). Place the ingredients in the tub, and enter the bath with the intention of healing whatever needs healing for you and learning to trust again. As you soak, close your eyes and envision a manatee swimming through the sea, emanating incredible loving grace into the water. Feel that energy surround you. Let it remind of you of the beautiful potential for love. Spend as much time as needed in the bath meditating and asking your heart what it needs to trust. When you're done, light a candle and journal about your bath experience and how you can continue to open your heart to love.

SACRED BONES

In shamanic and spiritual traditions, animal bones are sometimes used as ritual objects because they hold life energy within them. Indigenous Tainos would work with the supernatural essences and water wisdoms of the manatee by using a manatee rib bone in their sacred ceremonies.

MONKEY

PLAYFULNESS • LETTING GO • JOKESTER • MISCHIEVOUS • RESPONSIBILITY • SALVATION • AGILITY • LEADERSHIP • MAGNETISM

WHEN TO WORK WITH ME:

When you want to get along with a group, when you're ready to lead, when you're moving into a new home or making a big change, when you want to be more playful and fun, when you need to make fast and clear decisions, when you want to take on more responsibility or leadership

ENERGY MEDICINE:

Be ready for the unexpected. Oftentimes my medicine foretells of something surprising heading your way.

I bring forward strong abilities to change course at any needed time, to lead with a sense of play versus seriousness, and to make decisions with confidence and honor. Which of these aspects speaks most loudly to you?

If you are drawn to my energy, it may be time for you to step into greater leadership.

Remember that people are drawn to you for a reason. Go inward and ask yourself what inner quality attracts people to you.

Are you moving into a new home or a new chapter in your life? Call upon me to approach this transition with lightheartedness, ease, and a sense of fun.

What experience would energize your soul? I call on you to step out of your comfortable routine and explore an adventure, big or small, that will enliven your life.

POWER PRACTICE:

In this practice, we'll explore monkey energy by embracing lightheartedness and play. Get a pen and a piece of paper or your journal, and find a comfortable place sit. Draw seven trees in a row on the page, then close your eyes and gently connect with your breath and heart center. Now envision a line of seven trees in a lush jungle. Watch as a healthy, happy monkey moves from tree to tree, swinging from vines and branches as it makes its way through the forest. Notice how it moves with playful, curious energy. Invite monkey energy into your being. Relax your face muscles and your shoulders. Let go of tension and seriousness you're holding in your body. When the monkey has reached the final tree, open your eyes and ask yourself how you can introduce more play into your life. Using a stream-of-consciousness style of writing, write the first thing you think of beneath the first tree you drew. Then, like the monkey, move with ease to the second tree and write another thing that will bring more joy and play into your life. And so on, until all seven trees are filled out. When you're done, ask that monkey continue to empower you to manifest these things in your life. Make play a priority.

HANUMAN, THE MONKEY GOD

The monkey god Hanuman is one of the most respected deities in Hinduism and an important character in the Sanskrit epic *Ramayana*, a sacred text in Hinduism. There are Hanuman temples throughout India, where the monkey god is worshipped for his strength and energy. The areas around these temples are often informal sanctuaries for monkeys, safe spaces where they cannot be harmed.

MOOSE

SELF-ESTEEM • SOUL RETRIEVAL • FEMININE POWERS • TRAVERSING INNER AND OUTER WORLDS • CHILDHOOD • WISE WARRIOR • COSMIC CONNECTION

WHEN TO WORK WITH ME:

When you want to enhance your self-esteem and self-honor, when you want to heal from childhood wounds, when you want to operate from a place of deep wisdom, when you want to explore your metaphysical depths and abilities

ENERGY MEDICINE:

I am greatly skilled in healing childhood wounds or trauma; call upon me to further guide you in this process.

My medicine helps to balance deep inner work with the outer world around you. Work with me in shamanic processes such as soul retrieval.

I am here to remind you of your ability to connect in a big way with Great Spirit and Source. My powerful antlers act as vast antennas to these unseen realms.

My grounded and poised wisdom can bring you a richer embodiment of self-esteem. Call upon me to work with you when you need to build confidence.

Remember to appreciate, value, and honor yourself. Do not diminish or belittle your gifts or aspects of your personality. Allow yourself to be rooted in knowing your sacredness.

You entered this world with spiritual abilities. Trust in yourself to learn how to properly hone these gifts and stay strong as you step further into these realms again. Allow me to support you.

POWER PRACTICE:

Moose represents connecting to the depths of Earth and the heights of the cosmos. In this practice, we'll work on how to balance grounding energy with cosmic power. Find a quiet place to sit with your eyes closed. Picture a giant moose standing in a pond. Watch as it dips its great body, submerging its antlers, head, and shoulders into the water, gathering food for nourishment. Holding this image in your mind, feel your own energy going deep into the earth, connecting with the solidness of Great Mother Earth. Feel how this connection provides support and grounding.

Then, picture the moose's strong body rising back up. Watch as its massive antlers break the surface of the water and move up toward the sky. These are antennas and receivers of great cosmic wisdom from the Universe. Holding this image in your mind, send your energy flowing up toward the cosmos. Notice how the quality of this energy differs from and complements the grounding energy of Earth. Sit with this until you feel balanced—grounded and cosmic, all at once.

To manifest this grounding and cosmic energy in your everyday life, choose an item to represent each experience: Earth and cosmos. To represent Earth, you might choose a rock, a jar of sand, or a shell. For the cosmos, maybe it's a bowl of rain water or an image of the sun. Whatever feels right for you. Place these items on your altar or in a sacred space in your home. Call upon moose and these two objects to help strike divine balance.

MOSQUITO

BIRTH • CLEARING ENERGY • VIGILANCE • SMALL BUT PROFOUND • FOUNDATIONAL CHANGE • PERSPECTIVE • RESOLVING

WHEN TO WORK WITH ME:

When you want power over your emotions and small annoyances, when you want to clear energy suckers from your life, when you want to skillfully navigate big change, when you want a positive attitude and mindset, when you want to stop taking things too seriously

ENERGY MEDICINE:

When I show up, I often foretell of great, foundational change that will be occurring in your life. Remember, all is meant to serve and ascend you.

Are you making a big deal out of a small irritation? Remember not to take life too seriously. Check in with yourself to see if you're seeing things with a victim's perspective.

Is there a person or situation that is an energy drain for you? Be aware of things that continuously take, without giving much in return.

You are in control of your emotions. No matter what is going on around you, you have the ability to choose how you respond.

If you're experiencing challenge or annoyance, I can help you frame things in a better mindset. There may be an unexpected opportunity presenting to you right now. How is this experience making you stronger?

POWER PRACTICE:

Mosquito may be very small, but its medicine is enormous. Often mosquito presents as a power animal in your life when you are going through a period of change or dealing with a challenging situation. In this brief practice, close your eyes and imagine yourself as a mosquito hovering above your body, taking stock of your current situation. What can you see when you zoom out and take things in from the perspective of mosquito? Have the annoyances or changes in your life clouded your ability to see the bigger picture? Are you letting the little things hold you back? Hover for a while, seeing things from all angles and taking everything in. Then, return to your earth body and consider how you can reframe your mindset, based on what mosquito revealed.

ANNOYING AND ESSENTIAL

Mosquitos may seem irritating, but they are vital to our ecosystems, serving as pollinators for a wide variety of flowers and plants, and as food for thousands of animals.

MOTH

NURTURING • SCENT • CLOSURE • OPTIMISM • ATTRACTION • FAITH • DARK TO LIGHT • MOON AND STARS

WHEN TO WORK WITH ME:

When you want to realize what you need to let go of, when you're ready for closure, when you want to transform shadow energy or clear your energy field, when you want to remain optimistic, when you want to move toward what is positive for you and your life

ENERGY MEDICINE:

What shadow aspect—the dark, hidden parts of you—in your life is ready to be brought to light? Call me in for guidance in this healing revelation.

I bring potent medicine of keeping the faith. Continue moving forward, following the path you've set for yourself. This is your call to stay strong and keep going.

I am here to remind you of the power of attraction. The energy, chemistry, and scent you experience with another will often provide you with essential partnership wisdom.

Is there something gradually dissolving in your life? A relationship, a passion, a goal? Take a moment now to pause and reflect on what is trying to release and how that makes you feel. It's OK to let it go.

When challenge or difficult revelations arise, remember that you must navigate all the way through these processes in order to be reborn. Facing things honestly will allow you to eventually find liberation and joy.

POWER PRACTICE:

Moths are most active at night, guided by light from the moon and stars. For this practice, you will tune in to the guidance of the glowing celestial bodies in the night sky. Go outside when it's dark out and find a safe, comfortable place where you can sit or lie and gaze up at the night sky. Take a moment to be in awe of the universe. Then call upon moth to join you now. Envision a moth flying up toward the sky to greet the stars and moon. Once the moth is fluttering high above you, ask, "Beautiful stars and moon, is there anything you would like me to know?" Allow moth to relay the messages from these cosmic bodies. Listen. When you've finished gazing at the sky, envision the moth making its way back down to you on Earth. Ask moth to support you in heeding the messages you received.

INTERPRETATIONS OF MOTH COLORS

The moth's spiritual embodiment is spoken of in Polynesian mythology, where a black moth symbolizes the soul of man. The Goajiro of Colombia believe that if you find a large white moth in the bedroom, you must treat it with respect, as it is one of your ancestors coming to visit in spirit form.

MOUNTAIN GOAT

INTEGRITY • STURDINESS • PERSISTENCE • AMBITION • STEADY RISING • INDEPENDENCE • DILIGENCE • CONFIDENCE • SELF-ESTEEM • SEXUAL INTEGRITY

WHEN TO WORK WITH ME:

When you want to reach a lofty goal with a strong foundation and confidence, when you want to get out of a rut, when you want to strengthen your determination and ambition, when you want to have healthy sexual relations, when you're ready to break out of your comfort zone

ENERGY MEDICINE:

Is it time for you to take your confidence to new heights? I represent embarking on new endeavors and setting higher goals.

I am here to remind you of the deep power of trusting yourself to land on your own feet, no matter how big the jump.

Virility is one of my main medicines. I recommend keeping an honest, conscious awareness around your sexual experiences. Make sure these experiences are conducted with sacredness and honor.

Call upon me to empower you if you fear going back to old ways. I work to ensure that you move steadily up, without retreating.

It's time to explore new ways, new feelings, and new experiences in life. I empower you to open up to infinite possibilities and stay agile as you navigate higher and higher through new terrain.

POWER PRACTICE:

In this practice, you'll work with mountain goat medicine to actualize a new goal. Close your eyes and envision a tall mountain with a zigzag path to the top. At the top of this mountain is a big goal you hold in your heart.

Call upon mountain goat to work with you in getting clear on the steps you need to take to reach the summit. What actions, experiences, plans, or conversations are necessary for you to achieve your goal? Visualize each one of these steps as a point on the zigzag path up the mountain. Now, imagine a goat at the very bottom of the mountain, and watch as it begins to make its way up the path, moving through the steps with confidence. Watch as it moves higher and higher, even as the path gets steeper and harder. Stay until the goat reaches the summit. Then, open your eyes and thank mountain goat for showing you confidence, diligence, and integrity. Regularly return to this visualization as you work on persisting toward your goal.

EXPERT CLIMBERS

True to their medicine of persistence and determination, mountain goats have evolved to live in high-altitude environments, with hooves suited for navigating steep cliffs and rock faces. Their cloven hooves provide balance, and their soft foot pads provide traction and grip on tricky terrain; a mountain goat can jump more than 10 feet [3 m] in a single leap.

MOUNTAIN LION

EYE ON THE PRIZE • PROTECTION • HEALTHY BOUNDARIES • LEADERSHIP • FIRE AND SUN • WISDOM

WHEN TO WORK WITH ME:

When you need to be empowered as a leader, when you're ready to actualize a goal using higher wisdom, when you want extra protection and strength, when you need to soothe your anxieties, when you need to balance mind, body, spirit, and soul

ENERGY MEDICINE:

When being a leader feels challenging, call upon me to provide extra fortitude and remind you that natural leadership abilities exist deep within you.

I remind you that the greatest form of leadership comes from the heart and personal embodiment of the teachings you are sharing. Strong leadership does not come from force.

Leadership is not about trying to convince others to also join. It's simply about taking a stand for what you believe in and speaking and acting with honesty and heart.

I can calm your anxieties by bringing you back to what is really important and reminding you of the higher truth of your mission.

I hold the power of the fire and sun within me. If you are seeking clarity for next steps in your life, work with these elements—spend time in the sun or near a fire and ask it to illuminate your path.

My medicine helps you set intentions and maintain focus. Take time now to get clear on where you're heading, why, and how you want it to feel when you get there.

POWER PRACTICE:

In this practice, we'll work with mountain lion's leadership medicine. Gather a piece of paper and a pen, and find a quiet place to sit. Light a candle, close your eyes, and call sacred mountain lion in to work with you for this exercise. Breathe deeply as you feel mountain lion's energetic presence, its raw power and confidence filling the room. Now speak the following phrase out loud, "Dear mountain lion, what are four qualities that allow me to be a strong leader?" Remember, leadership can show up in many ways—it can be strong, it can be compassionate, it can be encouraging. Give yourself a few moments to consider what you offer as a leader. As the answers flow in, open your eyes and begin to write your list down on the piece of paper. When you've finished, place this list in a sacred place, such as your altar or on your dresser, where you'll see it every day. Refer to it any time you need to remember that you have natural leadership qualities within you.

MOUSE

DETAILS • SCRUTINY • FEAR • INSIGNIFICANCE • INSIGHT • FOCUS • ATTENTION • SURVIVAL

WHEN TO WORK WITH ME:

When you need to focus, when it's time to get out of survival mode, when you need to think outside the box, when you want to let go of old stories and emotions, when you want to release stress, when you want to reconnect to your power

ENERGY MEDICINE:

I am here to usher you into exploration of your realities. What stories about yourself or your life are outdated? What narratives are holding you back? Confront your current states so you can expand.

If you are faced with a challenge right now, my medicine urges you to dive deep into radical creative insights and solutions. It's time to think outside the box.

When I show up in your life it is likely because you are scurrying around and losing focus. This approach is creating an air of confusion. Taking a moment to refocus will serve you.

Are you operating in survival mode? If your sense of security is feeling shaky or threatened, making some time to identify and heal your wounds will empower you greatly.

My medicine will help you overcome resentment, anger, and fear. Hanging on to these emotions is debilitating. Calm your central nervous system, and once you're back into divine alignment, see what you can let go of.

I am here to remind you that you are a unique child of the cosmos, powerful beyond measure and infinite in your capacity to experience miracles.

POWER PRACTICE:

Mouse represents nervous, scattered energy, which can cause anxiety and prevent you from staying focused on working toward your dreams. When you feel pulled in a million directions, you're unable to give quality attention to any one thing, and you end up shortchanging the people around you, the projects you're working on, and yourself. Devoting time to just one fulfilling activity will help you reset and re-center. For this practice, set aside 2 full hours where you can commit to doing just one thing, something that you do *just for you* to clear stress and restore you in your power. You can sing, dance, enjoy time in nature, have a conversation with a loved one, spend time in prayer, perform an act of service—pick something that brings you joy. No phone, no computer, no distractions. Give the activity your full attention and commit to being 100 percent present. Afterward, spend some time in meditation considering how it felt to give all your attention to one thing. How can you bring that quality of attention and intention into other areas of your life?

MULTITASKING • GENIUS • HEALING • MYSTERIOUSNESS • REGENERATION • UNIQUENESS • LOOSENING UP • INFINITE EVOLUTION • FLOW

WHEN TO WORK WITH ME:

When you need to multitask, when you want to experience life with more grace and ease, when you need to heal something, when you need to loosen up, when you want to be alluring, when you're ready to be independent, when you want to connect to the mystical dance of the universe

ENERGY MEDICINE:

My medicine evokes the mystical dance you are taking part in as an ever-evolving human on an ever-evolving planet within the ever-evolving cosmos. Tune in to this.

Watch the way I dance with the sea to relearn how to flow. Are you moving gracefully through your life and surrendering to what you cannot control? Or are you resisting?

I remind you to give thanks for the miracles in your body. Your blood, skin, bones, organs, hair, breath—all are miraculous.

I call on you to trust your intuition when it's telling you what to let go of. When you clear what no longer serves you (people, places, things), this opens up new glorious space for you to move into a revitalized and regenerated self and life.

If people are drawn to you and asking you for your time, my medicine will help you remain grounded and independent.

If you feel overwhelmed by tasks, lists, or responsibilities of any sort, call upon me to elevate your ability to multitask with ease.

POWER PRACTICE:

Find a comfortable, quiet place to sit. Close your eyes and begin to imagine yourself as wise and ethereal octopus. Envision your eight swirling octopus arms extending from your body and slowly unfurling around you. Feel the water moving along your skin, renewing and cleansing you. Now ask yourself, "What would most fuel my beautiful soul right now?" Imagine that object, word, or symbol appearing in the water in front of you, and allow your octopus arms to reach out, grab it, and bring it toward your body. Next, ask, "What would allow me to become one with my highest spiritual powers?" See the answer appear in front of you, and have a second arm reach out to grab it and bring it back toward your body. Finally, ask, "What deep wisdom am I ready to share with the world?" Bring that answer in using another arm. Holding these three answers close to you, float with this amazing fuel for a moment. Finally, move through the water on a beautiful swim as you consider how to incorporate these learnings into your life. Open your eyes, and thank octopus for aiding you on this journey.

ANCIENT AND INTELLIGENT

The octopus is an ancient invertebrate—the oldest octopus fossil discovered dates back almost 300 million years. These wondrous sea creatures have eight legs, three hearts, and large brains that allow the animals to problem solve, complete puzzles, and move through mazes.

OSTRICH

DIGESTION • APPLIED KNOWLEDGE • GROUNDEDNESS • FERTILITY • SECRET POWERS AND ABILITIES

WHEN TO WORK WITH ME:

When you need to be present, when you need protection from drama or stress, when want to call more fertility into your life, when you want to feel grounded, when you want to apply cosmic knowledge in your daily life, when you want to raise your frequency and consciousness, when you want to process something big

ENERGY MEDICINE:

I remind you of the importance of staying grounded while connecting to cosmic realms. The key to finding your power is bringing cosmic spiritual energies back down to Earth.

I represent consciousness rising. Work with me to apply new heightened wisdom and awareness in very practical ways.

I lay the biggest egg in the world and bring powerful fertility medicine. Call upon me to bring fertile blessings to any area of your life.

I remind you that being humble and observant holds power; you do not need to bring big energy to every situation. Reserve your mind-blowing capabilities and charms for when you truly feel it's time to share.

If you are being pulled into stressful situation, it is best not to get involved. Remain in your power and do not get pulled into anyone else's drama.

My medicine will help you overcome perceived limitations. If you feel less-than or stuck, consider how you can pivot to use your unique powers and abilities to move forward.

POWER PRACTICE:

The ostrich is the world's largest bird, yet it does not have the ability to fly. This might cause some to think the bird is limited, but that belief would be deeply mistaken. The ostrich is a strong, magnificent bird with powerful legs that can run over 40 miles [64 km] per hour and kill an animal with one swift kick. In this practice, you will focus on overcoming perceived limitations so you can realize more of your hidden mega powers.

Gather your journal and a pen, find a quiet place to sit, and call on powerful ostrich to work with you. In your journal, write down something that you feel is holding you back or a belief about yourself that is limiting you. Now envision a giant ostrich running at top speed. Envision it kicking its powerful legs. Then, holding the giant ostrich in your mind, dive deeper into the limiting scenario you're facing and see whether you can find the hidden strengths that can help you overcome this particular problem. Ask yourself whether the things you're telling yourself are actually true. Oftentimes, our victim mindset or our subconscious tells us a false narrative that becomes part of our story. See whether you can flip the script and turn what you've been thinking is holding you back into one of your greatest secret strengths. Ask ostrich to remain with you in activating these new beliefs.

A SYMBOL OF FERTILITY AND REGENERATION

Residents of the oldest city in sub-Saharan Africa, Djenné (in present-day Mali), celebrate the ostrich as symbolizing fertility and regeneration. The spires of the city's great mosque, a World Heritage site, are covered with sculptures of ostrich eggs (ostrich eggs are the largest eggs on Earth). Each year, residents of Djenné take part in a festival to rebuild and restore the weathered mosque walls.

OWL

SEEING IN THE DARK • PSYCHIC AWARENESS • REINCARNATION • TRUTH BEYOND • DELUSION • DEEP LEARNING • OBSERVATION • FOREWARNING (OR PROPHECY) • HIDDEN KNOWLEDGE

WHEN TO WORK WITH ME:

When you need to see through deception, when you want to see beyond people's masks, when you're ready to face illusions and shadows, when you want to awaken your seer abilities, when you're experiencing a death and rebirth, when you want to do shadow work, when you want to awaken esoteric wisdom

ENERGY MEDICINE:

I remind you that though facing the dark truths and fears you've avoided can be overwhelming, the miracles that come from this work are worth it. Work with me to make a commitment to seeing truth in all things.

I awaken psychic, esoteric, and spiritual gifts. When I reveal myself, your mystical abilities are coming alive.

I am appearing because your observations and psychic sight are operating at a higher level. Seeing the shadows may at first feel scary, but it is in this transcendent place that you enter into miraculous living.

You may be entering a time of deep wisdom learning and increased awareness. As you move through this process, the key is to trust yourself to handle the revelations and trust that this experience is serving the highest, greatest, earthly good.

If you are experiencing a time where a part of you is dying off—a way of seeing things, an attachment, a dream—know that a rebirth and new liberation is imminent. Call upon me to help guide you through this seemingly treacherous terrain.

POWER PRACTICE:

Owl sometimes gets a bad reputation as the bringer of bad omens because of its ability to navigate between realms, boldly delivering messages, awareness, and wisdom. In fact, owl will take you to places that may be very difficult or uncomfortable in order to bring about positive transformation. This courageous medicine can profoundly change your life for the better because it frees you from delusions that create chaos, pain, and confusion. So, if you are willing to no longer be deceived, call upon great owl to work with you. Sitting or lying in a dark room with your eyes closed, envision an owl in a tree. Watch as the owl moves its head from side to side, almost in a full circle. Then envision the owl flying powerfully, silently, and with keen awareness into the night. Say out loud, "I allow this to be my wake-up call; I am willing to devote myself to truth." Ask owl's keen abilities to call forward any truth that you've previously ignored seeing. Make space for what arises. Owl medicine is very powerful, and the more you begin to appreciate living in a state of nondeception, the more you will begin to respect and celebrate the life-changing wisdoms it so generously and bravely imparts.

A SACRED BIRD

The owl is sacred in many ancient civilizations and religions. In Hinduism, the owl symbolizes the pursuit of knowledge in the darkness. In Greek mythology, what was known as the "owl of Athena" traveled with Athena, the goddess of wisdom. The white owl is especially sacred to the peoples of Siberia and Central Asia because it is said to have saved the life of Genghis Khan on more than one occasion.

"I recently traveled to Hawai'i to study Hawaiian culture and relationship with the *aina* (land or that which sustains us) with Aunty Mahealani Kuamo'o-Henry, a Kumu 'Elele o Na Kupuna, teacher and messenger of the ancestors. That's where I learned of the aumakua (power animals) that you may partner with if it is in highest alignment with your path.

"One day, Aunty suggested we have class with Na Kupuna (the ancestors) and to go where the island called us. We drove across Big Island to an ancestral sacred site. During our drive, we felt a moment of magnificence as we approached our halfway point, alongside Mauna Kea (a culturally and spiritually significant mountain).

"'Wait, wait. Stop the car!' my friend shouted. I pulled over and there was a newly dead pueo (owl). We felt we were supposed to prepare a proper burial to send our owl relative off in a good way. We placed it on a grassy patch nearby and created an altar with flowers, tobacco, and a medicine wheel of branches. We oriented the pueo to the east so its spirit would return home at sunrise. We asked permission from the pueo's spirit to receive one feather apiece as a gift and reminder of this sacred exchange—truly a ho'ailona (omen). We felt it was agreed upon, and we each carefully plucked one feather.

"I have had this feather on my altar ever since and have been physically visited by pueo at key moments, either before or after ceremony. It is a budding relationship that unfolds with time and humility, flying wing-to-wing with pueo and Great Spirit."

—Giuliano Geronymo
SHAMANIC SOUND HEALER

PEACOCK

SHINING AUTHENTICALLY • CLAIRVOYANCE • AURIC FIELD • PLAY • INTEGRITY • REBIRTH • SELF-LOVE

WHEN TO WORK WITH ME:

When you're ready to cultivate self-love, when you want creative inspiration, when you're ready to shine bright, when you're ready to open your third eye, when you're ready for a rebirth

ENERGY MEDICINE:

I evoke a powerful level of true self-love, balanced with beautiful humility. I remind you to share your true colors and gifts proudly to the world: It is why you are here.

When you need to lighten up and remember nothing should be taken too seriously, ask me for assistance. I help you remember to play.

I can activate your clairvoyant and psychic gifts. My feathers can clear your auric field and provide protective healing energies.

Call upon me when you want to ramp up your creative juices and expression.

Integrity, honor, and trustworthiness are a few of my main medicines—work with me to bring these attributes more alive within you and your life.

My annual molting symbolizes resurrection and renewal. When you are going through a time of growth or rebirth, call on me and I will help make things as graceful and smooth as possible.

POWER PRACTICE:

In this practice, you'll tap into the inspired, creative energy of peacock. Find a comfortable place to sit or lie down. Close your eyes and envision a peacock's tail with its brightly colored feathers displayed as a wide fan. Let your gaze wander along the dazzling blues and greens. Holding this image in your mind, ask yourself, "What creative abilities of mine want to be expressed? How can I share my true colors with the world?" Make note of any images, feelings, and words that come to mind. Pay attention; whatever comes up will help you unite with your soul. Like peacock, which is not afraid to display its authentic power, use this practice to explore untapped abilities and inner powers that you want to make come more alive.

SPECTACULAR TAILS

Peacocks' remarkable, iridescent tail feathers are used to attract mates. Their tails are made up of as many as 150 feathers that can grow up to 6 feet [1.8 m] in length, with each feather featuring a signature eyelike spot called an *ocellus* (derived from the Latin word for "eye"). The feathers are shed toward the end of summer, after mating season.

"I have always felt drawn to peacocks; their regal colors remind me of my Persian and Indian ancestors, their elegance and grace, their fierceness and power. Though they are beautiful, you also don't mess with a peacock. I love that duality.

"Several years ago, after living in New Delhi for two years, I could feel it was time for me to leave. I needed change; the trajectory of my life was not in alignment with my truth and I needed to take the quest to understand the depth of my soul.

"Around this time, I became extremely ill and couldn't leave my bed for days. In a hazy fog, I looked outside, and there was a great blue peacock staring at me through the window, a highly unusual sight in the middle of the bustling city of Delhi. It looked at me with its penetrative eyes and I knew it was communicating with me that it was time to spread my wings, find the power within me, and take off on the journey of my dharma, my soul's purpose.

"The peacock came to remind me to claim my majesty and rock the vibrant rainbow within. The peacock has taught me to unapologetically let my colors show in their unique radiance. It has also reminded me that you can live your fullest expression and have boundaries."

—Sahara Rose

SPIRITUAL TEACHER AND AUTHOR OF *DISCOVER YOUR DHARMA*

PENGUIN

DIMENSIONAL TRAVEL • SACRIFICE • DREAM STATE • RESPECT • BALANCE • ASTRAL TRAVEL • MONOGAMY

WHEN TO WORK WITH ME:

When you are looking for a monogamous relationship, when you need balance in life, when you want to receive messages in your dreams, when you need strength to make sacrifices, when you want to be respected or give more respect, when you need a dose of optimism

ENERGY MEDICINE:

Harmony is available to you. When you are moving through a challenging time or situation, remember that the discomfort will not last forever. Brighter times are ahead.

Balance is the name of my game. I represent the yin-yang energy system. What aspect of your life can you bring more into balance at this time?

If you're prepared to shed and sacrifice some things in order to live your absolute best in life, I am your medicine. I help you gain clarity when you ask yourself, "What can I sacrifice today in order to receive my ultimate dreams later?"

Who in your life could you give greater respect to? If you have been harsh with another (or yourself) recently, take a moment to investigate where that is coming from. Treat all beings with respect and honor.

Are you calling in a monogamous partnership? If so, I am your guide. Call upon me to help connect you with an aligned being looking for the same.

I represent out-of-body experiences, astral travel, and lucid dreaming. Be aware of what messages are trying to present to you via the unseen realms. Keep a dream journal when you're working with my energy.

POWER PRACTICE:

Penguins can powerfully propel themselves out of water and into the air with enough velocity and speed to keep them airborne for a few seconds. This represents the ability to transition with quickness and ease from one state or realm to the next. In this practice, you will work with penguin to activate the dream realm and achieve lucid dreams—the experience of knowing you're dreaming and being able to have some control over the experience. If you are at a place of readiness to awaken these spiritual gifts, call upon penguin to join you in this practice. Keep a dream journal next to your bed, and before you drift off to sleep, visualize a penguin leaping out of the water and invite penguin's guidance and medicine into your dreams. Be sure to record any dreams in your dream journal as soon as you wake. (To achieve lucid dreams, it may also help to set an alarm for early in the morning, get up and get a glass of water, and then get back in bed and let yourself drift back to sleep—people often experience lucid dreams during this second sleep.)

PIG

GOOD FORTUNE • EARTH ABUNDANCE • SELF-WORTH • CALMNESS • SMARTS • RENEWAL • SINCERITY • YOUTHFULNESS

WHEN TO WORK WITH ME:

When you want to attract sincere people, when you want to be more generous, when you want steady financial wealth, when you want to have a foundation of abundance, when you want a balance between relaxation and passion, when you want to clear scarcity mentality, when you want to be unaffected by the opinions of others

ENERGY MEDICINE:

I call upon you to be more generous. Tune in to the abundance in your life and consider how you can bestow some of your wealth onto another. This does not just apply to financial wealth; remember, there are many generous gifts you can share with the world.

My social, cuddly energy reminds you of the power of bonding with loved ones. Reach out to cherished friends and family and make time for true connection and intimate conversation.

I remind you not to judge a book by its cover. Just because someone is choosing to live in a way that is vastly different from the way you live does not make them wrong. Keep a sincere, open heart. Let people walk their own paths.

I activate a "know thyself" power that allows you to be unbothered by other people's opinions and judgments.

I help you feel align with success in all its forms. Call on my energy to cultivate a healthy and balanced relationship to wealth. Unite with me to clear fear of scarcity. There will always be enough for you.

POWER PRACTICE:

In this practice, you'll tap into pig's medicine of sincerity, warmth, and generosity. Close your eyes and imagine a group of pigs in a large pen. Hear the playful sounds of pigs snorting as they communicate with one another. Envision them having not a care in the world while they frolic in the mud and cuddle together in their pen. Now think about someone in your life who would benefit from quality time with you. Who is the first person that comes to mind? It's time to reach out to them. Make a plan to spend time together, just the two of you, without distractions. Time where you sincerely share feelings from your heart. Create an environment and energy of warmth for them to feel appreciated and safely held within your friendship. Allow yourself to be grateful for this abundance of love and connection. Repeat this practice whenever you're in need of bonding experiences.

PORCUPINE

TRUST • VULNERABILITY • WONDERMENT • DEFENSES • ANCESTORS • INNOCENCE • LIGHTHEARTEDNESS • HUMILITY • HEALTH

WHEN TO WORK WITH ME:

When you need a break from the stresses of adulthood, when you want to reconnect to the joys of childhood, when you want to connect with your ancestors, when you want to take care of your body and eat well, when you want to let your defenses down, when you want to trust again

ENERGY MEDICINE:

Are you wanting to trust again? Healing the place where trust was initially shut down will serve you. Learning to trust once more allows others to fully share the love they want to give to you.

I call for you to remember what gave you the most joy as a child. Returning to these pure places will unite you further with your soul.

Have words or criticisms from others affected you? Is there something someone said or did that you need to finally let go of? Take your power back and remember who you are.

If you have been the one saying things with a sharp edge to it, it is time to clear away the harsh charge and fill the space with a gentler energy.

When I present in your life, I am also a great reminder to honor your ancestors and what you are ingesting.

It is human nature to want to protect yourself; however, there is great power in examining the precise places where you still feel a need to defend yourself. Why are you so defensive? What is behind the defense? What are you trying to protect yourself from?

POWER PRACTICE:

In this practice, we'll tune in to the power of porcupine quills to answer burning questions. First, get your journal or a piece of paper and write down three pressing yes or no questions. These questions can be about love, career, friendship, dreams—whatever arises. Once you've written your questions, close your eyes and call porcupine forward in your mind. See its gray body, covered in spiky quills, move toward you. Begin asking porcupine your questions. If it raises its quills up straight, that means the answer is "Yes." If the quills remain flat, that means "No." Allow porcupine's highly attuned quills to be your navigation system for the clarity you seek! Once you've finished asking your questions, thank porcupine. Then, it's up to you to heed its wisdom.

PROTECTIVE QUILLS

The porcupine's quills are a physical manifestation of the animal's medicine of self-protection. When a porcupine feels threatened, it can shake its quills to make a rattling sound that warns predators. If a perceived predator comes close enough to touch the porcupine, the porcupine can release its quills, which are loosely attached to its body (they do not shoot the quills though, as many people believe). A porcupine can regrow the quills it has released.

PRAYING MANTIS

PRECISION • PROPHECY • CONTEMPLATION • DELIBERATION • VISION • PRAYER • PERCEPTION • SYNCHRONICITY

WHEN TO WORK WITH ME:

When you need to make wise choices, when you want to act with precision, when you want to deepen your mindfulness practice, when you need more patience, when you want to slow down and connect with inner wisdom, when you want to sharpen your clairvoyant abilities, when you want to do the greatest good

ENERGY MEDICINE:

Are you being too hasty with your actions or words? I teach you how to use the immense power of stillness to achieve clarity, which can then lead to action.

I am associated with rituals related to mindfulness and connecting to the unseen realms. Work with me when in prayer, meditation, or ancient healing arts to take your practice deeper.

If you want to sync up with and live by the rhythms and desires of your soul and body rather than external constructs like alarm clocks and forced work schedules, call upon my medicine to help guide you into this state of being.

Do not rush your next actions or speak of your visions too soon. Be patient and wait for the exact time to step forward or speak. You will know.

When I show up it is for a deep, divine reason. Inquire wholeheartedly within yourself what you feel I am here to teach you.

If you are seeking clarity in next steps or answers, surrender the issue or question to me, Great Spirit, and Great Mother Earth, releasing it and asking for the solution that serves the highest good to be revealed.

POWER PRACTICE:

In this practice, you will call upon revered praying mantis to help in decision-making. Praying mantis is a master of being still, waiting to strike at the *exact* precise moment. This practice should only be worked with when you are trying to make an important decision. When that decision is looming, call upon praying mantis to divinely guide you in clarity and timing. Close your eyes and watch a praying mantis. See how it observes from all angles and sometimes leans in ever so slightly to get an even clearer read on when the *precise* moment is to strike. Write down all of the possible options in this decision-making process. Say inwardly or aloud before each of those options, "Sacred praying mantis and my soul, is making the decision to _____ serving my highest good?" Directly after you ask, you will hear a "yes" or a "no." If all current possibilities receive a "no" answer, it is not the right time to make your move. Repeat this process when you have more possible answers or solutions. If a "yes" is revealed, this is divine guidance being provided, and it is then up to you to heed it and trust it is taking you to the highest possible next place for your life.

KUNG FU INSPIRATION

According to a legend from the late Ming/early Qing dynasties in China, the praying mantis inspired a form of Kung Fu, the Chinese martial art. In this legend, Wang Lang, a Kung Fu master from Shandong, lost a martial arts competition. After the loss, he went to rest under a tree. There, he watched a praying mantis trying to catch a cicada and was inspired by the agile moves of the mantis. It is said he then collected praying mantises and took them back to the Shaolin Temple to observe closely. He went on to create his own form of Kung Fu inspired by the mantis's moves.

RABBIT

QUICK DECISION-MAKING • SEIZING OPPORTUNITY • FERTILITY • LEAP OF FAITH • PLANNING • DIVINATION • OUTSMARTING • TRANSCENDING FEARS • THE MOON

WHEN TO WORK WITH ME:

When you want to seize an opportunity, when you want to activate a new life force, when you are entering a committed relationship, when you want to work with the cycles and power of the moon, when you're ready to face your fears, when you want to release stress

ENERGY MEDICINE:

I carry strong medicine of agile, fast, forward movement. Call upon my abilities when you need to act quickly and seize an opportunity.

Work with me during the new moon or the full moon. The benefits from rituals performed on these days will be amplified.

I carry strong sexual energy. I am a reminder to be mindful of how you carry and engage with intimacy. Are engaging in sacred experiences that honor your body and spirit?

I call on you to consider your faithfulness and commitment within relationships, and remind you that being faithful may involve some sacrifice.

I represent taking things to the next level. If you are ready to make moves, I am your guide.

What fears or anxieties have been holding you back? It's time to take an honest look at the stories that are preventing you from embracing radical transformation. Call on me in facing these darker emotions so that you can find true liberation.

If you have felt paralyzed or stuck, I bring with me a potent medicine to invigorate new life force. Work with me when you want to awaken your inner inspiration and fire at the precise divine time.

POWER PRACTICE:

For this practice, you will work with rabbit, fire, and the moon to take things to the next level in you life. During the next new or full moon, go outside with a candle, a blanket, a piece of paper, and a pen. Find a comfortable place to sit on your blanket, light your candle, and invite sacred rabbit to guide you in this ritual. Spend a few moments connecting to your breath, then write down one thing you want to breathe new life into. What do you want to take to the next level? Ask that rabbit bless this area of your life. Next, light the corner of the paper on fire and let it burn. Allow the sacred fire to activate your dream. Last, give yourself permission to move or dance around your candle, celebrating the new life force you've been graced with in this area of your life. Celebrate as if the thing you wrote down has *already* gone to the next level. Thank and honor rabbit, sacred fire, and the moon for working with you.

RABBITS IN ANCIENT BRITON

It is said that some ancient Britons relied upon the rabbit as a divination instrument. Studying the rabbit's feeding patterns, actions, and trails provided guidance in prophesying. Because of the rabbit's sacred role within the society, it was unlawful to eat them.

RACCOON

ENERGY HEALING WITH HANDS • CURIOSITY • CHANGE • WATER PURIFICATION • SURRENDER • ACTION

WHEN TO WORK WITH ME:

When you want permission to change, when you want to see playful new options, when you want to awaken your healing abilities, when you want fierce determination to reach your goal, when you want to see through secrets or lies, when you want to be helpful

ENERGY MEDICINE:

My mask represents giving yourself permission to become what you want, to change. Tune in to the characteristics or abilities you desire and wear that mask until it becomes one with you.

I also bring forward the ability to reveal what is authentic and what is shrouded in secrets or lies. Call upon me to assist you in this discernment.

I embody the ability to heal, especially the ability to sense and transform energy through the hands. If you are feeling anxiety, work with water as soon as possible. Doing an energy-cleansing handwashing ritual or taking a healing bath will soothe you.

I represent a balance of surrender and action. I surrender first to Great Spirit and Source and ask to be shown which way forward will serve the greatest good; when I receive clarity, I move from there with fierce determination.

My heart sincerely loves to help. I awaken the ability within you to share offerings with the world that will both be of service and also bring you immense joy and satisfaction.

POWER PRACTICE:

Take a moment to focus on the face of our sacred raccoon friend here in this book, tuning in to all the details in its mask-like face. Now close your eyes, and take a moment to think about what positive emotion or personality trait you feel would most enhance your life. Optimism, joy, kindness, intelligence, curiosity, patience—whatever calls to you. Now, in your mind, imagine a mask that represents that trait or emotion. See it in front of you. Pick up the mask and slip it over your face. Notice how it feels to have this quality activated within you. Any time you are in a situation where you want to embody a trait you don't feel you already have, envision putting your sacred mask on and infusing yourself with those powers. If you do this practice regularly, eventually you will no longer need the mask, as you will fully embody the positive trait you invited in.

DOUSING

Raccoons carry tremendous power in their paws. Their hands have four times more sensory receptors than human hands. These receptors become even more powerful when the raccoon wets its paws, stimulating the nerve cells, in a process known as "dousing." Raccoons douse their food and paws in water to increase their tactile experience, which helps them feel whatever food they've picked up. Raccoons have poor eyesight, so dousing is almost like "seeing" with their paws.

RAVEN

DIVINE TIMING • SPIRITUAL LAW • MESSENGER • SHAPE-SHIFTING • MYSTICISM AND MAGIC • LANGUAGE • INTENTION • COMMUNICATION

WHEN TO WORK WITH ME:

When you want to be a better communicator, when you want to be in sacred alignment with the Universe, when you're ready to face darkness so that you can experience light, when you're ready for a shift in consciousness

ENERGY MEDICINE:

My powers are deep and vast. I teach how to enter the void and then bring back the wisdom needed to manifest what you want.

I am a master of divine creation. Some may fear my processes because I teach of going into the darkness to free more light. It is in this way that you become less afraid of the unknown and more connected to trusting the mysteries of life.

While I represent death and rebirth, this process is not to be feared. As one way dissolves, you are then in a new space to have a higher-aligned creation come forward.

When I call and come to you, I am delivering a specific message. Is this time in your life marking a profound turning point?

I bring forward energies of shifts in consciousness, awakenings, and intelligence. When I present, I carry information around magic and deep change occurring in your life.

It is time for you to embrace the profound wisdom and gifts that you carry. Call upon me to empower them within you.

POWER PRACTICE:

For this practice, you will look to raven, representing the creator of the Universe, and raven's iridescent black, blue, and green feathers, representing what emerges from the void. Gather black, blue, and green writing utensils and a sheet of paper. Light a candle and invite sacred raven to work with you in this practice. Begin to draw anything you want with black only, then do the same with the other colors. Once you are done drawing, meditate briefly on the black drawing first. Ask yourself, "What new universe do I want to create for myself from the healing powers of this color?" Write all that comes up around the black drawing. Do the same process for the blue drawing and the green drawing. Keep this on your altar or in a sacred place and call raven in to be with you to birth this new universe to serve the greatest good of all. Observe where you are guided, what new ideas come to you, and what happens in the weeks and months ahead.

RAVEN THE CREATOR

To the Tsimshian, Indigenous people of the northwest coast of North America, primarily British Columbia and Alaska, the raven is seen as the creator of the Universe and an animal that acts as a bridge between the physical and spiritual realms. Similarly, the Inuit of Greenland and the Canadian Arctic see the bird as "raven father," creator of all life.

"When I began my journey into the ways of Daoist shamanism, my teacher said, 'You are embarking on the journey home. This is a spiritual journey, and the spiritual journey is a mystical one.' I was taught Daoist meditation techniques and practices to help face fears and expand consciousness, and to connect with the elemental and nature spirits. After one of these lessons, my left brain, the realm of logic and reason, began to question what I was being taught. As I was reflecting on this, Spirit gifted me with the proof I was seeking.

"I pulled into the driveway of my house in upstate New York, and as I got out of my car, I felt a powerful force approaching behind me. Time and space stood still, and I was filled with an intense connection to the field of energy coming toward my back. I couldn't physically move, but I could hear the flapping of powerful wings. It felt as if nothing else existed. Before I could turn to see what it was, the presence brushed its mighty wing across the right side of my head. It was a magnificent raven. The sacred creature flew past me, then turned around and headed right back toward me, landing on the roof of my house.

"My eyes filled with tears and my heart beat hard as we looked into each other's eyes and connected soul to soul. In what seemed like an eternity, but was probably a few seconds, this mysterious creature and I bonded. I experienced a communication with it that transcended physical reality. What was shared in that initiation was that I needed to get out of my head. I literally needed to stop the left-brain activity and engage more with the right brain, the realm of magic and mystery, the home of the raven.

"This is why the raven touched the right side of my head: to remind me of the other half. I was filled with a sense of trust and support and such gratitude for my beloved teacher, whose teaching was repeated to me by the raven: 'Reason and rationale are the antagonists to magic.' Since connecting with the raven as my power animal and sacred ally, its magical presence has continued to support my shamanic journey.

"I recommend connecting with the raven as a power animal for anyone interested in magic, and especially for anyone on the path of self-discovery. Both processes involve delving deep into the unknown and the mysterious, and can at times feel lonely, isolating, and hopeless. Raven has a powerful vibration of support during the dark times, especially when one feels alone. Raven's presence has dramatically improved my life by providing the confirmation I needed to believe in magic and the unknown.

"The darkness raven animates with its beautiful black feathers represents the void and the mystical aspects of reality. Nuummite, also known as the sorcerer's stone, is the perfect crystal to work with in meditation to connect to the raven. When there is a raven sighting, take a moment to connect to its palpable presence and feel it. Both practices will create a relationship with this extraordinary and magical creature. Raven is present to help us navigate through the mystery."

—Paul K. Alexander

DAOIST SHAMAN, ACUPUNCTURIST, AND ENERGY MEDICINE HEALER

RHINOCEROS

ANCIENT WISDOM • STABILITY • ABUNDANCE • WAKE-UP CALL • OVERCOMING OBSTACLES

WHEN TO WORK WITH ME:

When you want to blast through obstacles and level up (especially in your career), when you want to release procrastination, when you want more enlightenment in your life, when you want to be a magnet for abundance, when you need to be reminded that life is full of miracles

ENERGY MEDICINE:

I bring forth wisdom, success, and power in your chosen field. Staying in sync with the rhythms of our planet and nature will strengthen you.

I am also a bold and loud wake-up call—things are not as they seem. Are you judging yourself or a situation through an old lens?

Do you trust that all is miracle-filled and teaching and serving you? Do not let any obstacles stop you from reaching your goal.

Call upon me when you are looking for more confidence, sure-footedness, and stability.

I am known for assisting those ready to pierce the veil of illusion and I help provide enlightenment.

I remind you about how abundant your life is. Direct your attention to all the bounty that surrounds you.

POWER PRACTICE:

Rhinoceros reminds us that abundance, energy, and miracles are everywhere. This practice will return you to this truth. Find a place to sit comfortably, with a journal and pen by your side. Close your eyes and call for rhino to come forward to be with you in this practice. Envision rhino's powerful, majestic body ambling toward you. See its gorgeous horn and dark eyes. Then, take clearing, relaxing breaths for 3 minutes and think about the miracles surrounding you, the things you are grateful for, and the ways that abundance shows up in your life. Open your eyes and write down five miracles surrounding you, five things you are grateful for, and five ways your life is rich and abundant. If you have a crystal, place it on the list and allow the crystal to charge with the energy of your list. For the next 3 weeks, sleep with this list and the crystal near you or under your pillow. Before you go to bed each night, invite miracles to be revealed.

“It was a starry night and we were sitting around a fire in front of our lodge at a game reserve in Namibia. I’d already spotted heavily breathing hippos, a camouflaged crocodile, and too many kudus to count. In an effort to protect rhinos from poachers, signs prohibited us from photographing them. Hours went by with no rhinos in sight.

“And then . . . it appeared. Everything around the water hole seemed to freeze in awe of its majesty. What unfolded was a potent shift in perspective, a remembering that is still alive in my heart. As I watched the strong animal approach the water hole, it leaned toward the water as if it were looking at its own reflection. There was no space for judgment—only pure being. In that moment, I remembered my own unique nature and gifts, and was reminded to show up in the world just as I am.

"When you're looking to reconnect with your unique power and confidence, call upon rhino. It will remind you to stay connected to what feels alive in your energetic body without being distracted by what it looks like in the physical realm."

—Ksenia Avdulova

GUIDE FOR SPIRITUAL LEADERS

ROADRUNNER

SPIRITUAL PROTECTION • MENTAL POWER AND AGILITY • SPEED • TRANSFORMING ENERGY • GETTING UNSTUCK

WHEN TO WORK WITH ME:

When you want to stop procrastinating, when you want to change the energy within you or a room, when you want to make quick decisions with clarity, when you want mental strength, when you need to trust your gut, when you feel overwhelmed

ENERGY MEDICINE:

My medicine can change the energy of a space or room quickly. If you want to shift stagnant energy or you feel stuck in an emotion, call on me create transformation.

I am a master of thinking quickly on my feet, especially in the midst of change. I share with you the wise ways of making necessary pivots in life with divine precision.

I activate a deeper ability within you to trust in your innate wisdoms and intelligences. If you are pressed to make a quick decision, go with your gut and know you will find your way no matter what.

I can help you shift from procrastination to action, quickly. Call upon me to snap you out of being in a rut.

If you have started too many projects and are struggling to bring one all the way to fruition, call upon me to give you extra focus and determination.

I remind you of the importance of stability and balance as you are moving toward a goal. Imbalance can cause burnout and leave you feeling unfulfilled. Remember to tend to your mind, body, and soul as you work toward achieving your dreams.

POWER PRACTICE:

Roadrunner embodies intuition, action, and the courage to go after what you want. In this practice, you'll work on pursuing your goals with the energy of roadrunner. Find a comfortable place to sit, and close your eyes. Envision yourself in the desert, as a roadrunner in motion. Feel your fast-moving legs (able to run up to 20 miles [32 km] per hour) and your crown plumage reaching up toward the wisdoms of the sky, and see with your fiercely focused eyes. As you scan the horizon, visualize a large circle out in the distance, with one of your biggest goals sitting in the center. It could be a promotion, a romantic partnership, a financial goal. Whatever speaks to your soul in this moment. Observe this goal; feel the power of knowing that what you want is within sight. Now, go for it. Run, faster than you've ever run before, until you reach the circle. Dive in and grab your goal with your beak. It is yours. Now return to your physical body. When you are ready, open your eyes. Thank roadrunner for showing you the courage, action, and energy it will take to get what you want.

DISTINCTIVE TRACKS

Roadrunners have zygodactyl feet, which means two of their toes point forward and two point backward. Some members of the Hopi tribe in North America view this as a clever concealment, because their prints face both ways, making it difficult to tell which direction the bird is going and throwing bad spirits off track. Members of the Mogollon tribe in the American Southwest also revered the roadrunner, and the birds' distinctive tracks are found in their rock art.

ROOSTER
THRIVING • RESURRECTION • PROTECTION •
STAKING CLAIM • SOLAR POWER • FULL EXPRESSION •
JOY • HEALTHY RELATIONSHIPS

WHEN TO WORK WITH ME:

When you want supportive relationships, when you need to get in touch with your magnificence, when you want to expand your joy, when you want more ease and humor in your life, when you want clarity on intentions (yours and others'), when you want to have healthy relationships

ENERGY MEDICINE:

I remind you of the importance of cultivating relationships where you are able to be your full self. If you feel a relationship is keeping you from shining at your brightest, it may be time to reevaluate its place in your life.

Do not hold back your joy or enthusiasm. If you have been judged for having a vibrant personality, do not allow other people's criticisms to dim your light.

I help you become consciously aware of the intentions of those around you. This is your wake-up call to not allow anyone to take your power away from you.

Are you understanding the magnificence of you and your power? My medicine helps awaken you to the knowledge that you have the same energies within you that birthed the entire Universe. You are an infinite miracle.

I help you navigate through any life element free of despair or stress. Call on me to guide you with lightness, ease, and humor.

POWER PRACTICE:

In this practice, you will work with rooster to help you wake up to your unique gifts and powers. Find a place to sit or lie comfortably. Take a moment to envision a rooster. Really take it in and feel its confidence and full expression as it proudly struts in front of you. Hear its proud crow. Next, ask rooster to work with you as you close your eyes and connect with your heart and your breath. Take your attention down to your lower belly, where your creative center lives, and ask rooster to meet you there. Ask your lower belly, your sacral chakra, "What gift do I have inside of me that wants to express itself more in my life? What am I holding back because of fear of judgment or the fear that I am 'too much'?" Once you receive the answers, speak them loudly, like a rooster crowing. Do not hold back. Thank your body and soul wisdom for expressing to you and thank rooster for being your guide.

SALAMANDER

INNER FIRE • LEGENDARY • PURIFICATION • RITES OF PASSAGE • EMOTIONAL PATTERNS • PIVOTING • LUCID DREAMING

WHEN TO WORK WITH ME:

When you want to maintain a healthy mindset during a period of change, when you're ready to experience reverence and trust toward your emotions, when you're ready to break free of a pattern, when you want to burn away old aspects holding you back, when you want to embrace transformation

ENERGY MEDICINE:

I connect you with sacred fire. Are you ready to burn away what no longer serves you and transform through the energy of divine flames?

I bring forward the remembrance of the beauty in experiencing balance and knowing both ends of the spectrum, understanding both light and dark. If you are going through a rough time, rest assured that you'll emerge with the ability to expand into more reverence and joy in life.

Is there a certain emotional pattern you have observed about yourself? Are you stuck in an endless loop, one that you can't seem to escape? Call upon me to help you bring forward a new reality.

As transformation presents in your life, how much are you fighting the change and new flow? I teach adaptability and acceptance that evolution is one of the grandest aspects of life.

I remind you of the importance of treating your sacred environment, both at home and outside in nature, with respect and honor.

If you have set a vision that would require a new version of you in order to attain it, embrace when the spiritual fires roll in to burn away old aspects of you that are no longer needed.

POWER PRACTICE:

Salamander reminds us that even during intense fires of change, we can indeed remain cool, centered, and in our power. Collect a piece of paper and a pen, then close your eyes and connect with salamander. Notice its moist skin and its even breath. Open your eyes, and on a piece of paper, make two columns. At the top of the left column write "The Fires of Change" and at the top of the right column write "I Embody the Salamander." Now, in the left column, begin to list the things you're ready to let go of—anything toxic, old, or heavy that no longer supports your personal power. In the right column, list the ways you want to feel as you move through profound change in your life. Remember salamander's cool, centered energy. Really take your time with this practice and fill in the columns until you feel complete. Keep this piece of paper in a sacred place in your house, and when you're going through periods of change, take out the list, light a candle, and call in salamander to help you navigate the fires of change.

THE SALAMANDER AND FIRE

The salamander has long been associated with fire. The word *salamander* originates from the Persian words *sām*, meaning "fire," and *andarūn*, meaning "within." In ancient Greece and Rome, the salamander was believed to be a spirit that lived in fire. Aristotle and Pliny the Elder mention a legendary lizard that dwells in fire. The alchemists of the Renaissance believed the salamander represented a strong spiritual symbol for heat and fire giving new life. To the alchemists, fire did not symbolize destruction of new life; it released life.

SEAGULL

ENDURANCE • SURVIVOR MODE • REFINEMENT • RESPECT • CLEANING UP • AMBITION

WHEN TO WORK WITH ME:

When you want respect, when you don't want to settle for less than you deserve, when you want fresh energy, when you're ready to clear debris in your life, when you want to experience passion, when you want clear solutions, when you want confidence as you expand and grow

ENERGY MEDICINE:

I enter to remind you that you deserve to be treated with respect, and that same treatment is what is also right for others. Are there any relationships in your life where more respect is needed?

Take a look around your home and workspace to see whether there is any debris you can get rid of. See your space with a fresh set of eyes so the area can be freshened up too. This will open up new energy channels for your life that will serve you.

I bring forward a new sense of passion and long-standing drive for you. What is it that you want to really experience in this lifetime? Do not settle for less.

Remember that you have whatever it takes to rise to the occasion. If you are in an expansion experience, call upon me to empower you.

There are answers and solutions all around you. I am your reminder to never feel stuck or despairing. Work with me to allow the resources to be easily revealed.

I help awaken a sense of independence, intelligence, and embracing of your uniqueness within you. These are all traits I am highly skilled with.

POWER PRACTICE:

Seagulls are known for scavenging for food, clearing anything that's been left and picking it clean. For this practice, you will be cleaning up any mental debris that's holding you back. The limiting or negative beliefs we hold about ourselves can wreak havoc in our lives. It's time to work with seagull to clear these unhelpful self-judgments. On a piece of paper, draw three circles. Inside each circle, write a fear or limiting belief you are ready to clear. Call seagull forward, saying, "Dear and sacred seagull, I invite you in to work with me in energetically clearing these negative thoughts. I am ready to expand with new energy and grow with new confidence. Thank you for your support. And so it is." Now begin to rip up the paper while saying, "I trust in my highest destiny and know I am fully supported."

SEAL

IMAGINATION • INTUITION • HEART CONNECTION • SOUL TRUTH • SONG • MATERNAL HEALING • MYSTERY

WHEN TO WORK WITH ME:

When you want to improve your relationships, when you want to trust yourself to feel deeply, when you want to connect with chanting or song, when you want to open your imagination and creativity, when you want to heal a maternal relationship, when you want to hear your inner wisdom, when you want to awaken to the oneness of all that is

ENERGY MEDICINE:

Much of my medicine lives in the sounds I sing. Do you trust yourself to enter the waters of intimate emotions? When was the last time you let yourself swim in the dark abyss of your deepest feelings?

My songs will connect you to the deepest places within your soul.

I am known for my strength in awakening the powers of creativity and imagination. Call on me when you need to see something with fresh, dynamic energy.

When you're faced with a difficult decision, I will remind you of your innate wisdom and intuition. Let it guide you.

I represent tending to and healing relationships, especially pertaining to your mother (or a mother figure). Call upon me for guidance.

I remind you to cultivate love in your heart for all animals and humans. An open heart will open your life up to miracles beyond measure and deepest healing.

POWER PRACTICE:

Because seals have very powerful vision under water, they represent the ability to see your soul's truth. Close your eyes, and imagine you're a magnificent seal submerged in dark, cold water. Spend at least 5 minutes swimming as a seal. Begin to sing the seal's deep, vibrational song. As you swim, notice what thoughts and emotions come up. It may be overwhelming, but don't be afraid. These are the intimate truths of your soul. Notice what arises, without judgment, and continue swimming and singing. When you feel this process is finished, return to your body. Thank seal for taking you to the depths of your soul to reveal the deepest truths.

SHARK

NAVIGATION • CLEARING • FACING FEAR • RISING • BALANCE • HEIGHTENED SENSES • ELIMINATION • COMMUNICATION

WHEN TO WORK WITH ME:

When you need to navigate your fears, when you're ready to clear negative people or energy, when you want to have better work-life balance, when you want to be in tune with your emotions and communicate in a healthy way, when you want to be a pro at navigating life's journey

ENERGY MEDICINE:

Call upon me to clear negative people or discord from your life. Anything that is bringing bad energy can be cleared from your field with me by your side.

My sacred swim demonstrates how to navigate through life with skill and ease. I am a great teacher of being at one with all your Earth journeys.

I am your drama antidote. Work with me if you're ready to clear drama and any possible addiction you have to it.

My medicine reminds you of the importance of providing clear and calm communication, even if it is to alert another that your current state is unfavorable and you need some breath and space.

Be honest with yourself if your life is out of balance, especially when it comes to work. Are your relationships suffering because of your commitment to your career or professional pursuits? Call upon me to teach you how to achieve your dreams without doing harm to your personal life.

POWER PRACTICE:

This practice taps into shark's remarkable sensory abilities—a shark can smell just one drop of blood in the ocean and hear subtle sounds as far away as 800 feet [240 m]. Perform this practice when you are preparing to enter into a situation where you need to be as sharp and clear as possible. Take a moment to connect with shark by gazing at the illustration here in the book or closing your eyes and picturing a shark. Now call shark forward to work with you to help you bring more discernment to your life. Speak these words out loud: "Sacred shark, I call upon you to help activate within me a powerful ability to sense who and what will positively serve me and who and what I should avoid. Work with me to help me discern with ease and total clarity. And so it is." Carry this power with you into your day.

SHEEP

OPENHEARTEDNESS • WAKEFULNESS • PEACE • NOBILITY • GRATITUDE • SIMPLICITY • NAIVETY OR INNOCENCE • KINDNESS

WHEN TO WORK WITH ME:

When you want to act with an open heart, when you want to be awake to the world around you, when you want to bring people together, when you want to focus on global harmony, when you want to feel more gratitude, when you want to be less afraid, when you want to remain optimistic

ENERGY MEDICINE:

I am here to remind you that your gentleness, innocence, and vulnerability are beautiful qualities. Do not let the world harden you.

If you've been feeling extra sensitive, that's OK. Your vulnerable, open heart is a gift. Make sure you are surrounded by people who appreciate this quality in you. You deserve to be honored with unconditional love and respect.

Be pure with your golden heart, but be consciously aware and awake too. Do not let people take advantage of this sacred quality.

I represent an openness to new places and new adventures. My medicine will help you approach these opportunities with optimism and joy.

I bring medicine of unity and oneness. Work with me, and your good intentions and pure heart will make you an ideal person to bring people together in harmony and make everyone feel included.

POWER PRACTICE:

Sheep medicine is all about putting the *unity* in *community*, so for this practice you are looking at how to cultivate connections. Give yourself permission to spend 5 minutes sitting quietly and comfortably. Envision walking into a field where there are hundreds of sheep moving together in a herd. Now you see that there's one sheep all by itself, separated from the herd, looking alone and abandoned. As you walk toward this lone sheep, think of who you know who might be feeling this way right now. Who in your life may be by themselves, feeling alone and wishing they were experiencing more love and protection? Envision the person you thought of as this lonely sheep. Ask the sheep, "How can I better support you in feeling included, appreciated, and loved?" Ask this question as many times as needed until an answer reveals. Open your eyes, and commit to reaching out to the person who came to mind to offer them your kindness and love.

AN ANCIENT SYMBOL

Lambs were sacred animals in many ancient cultures, including in Sumer, a region of Mesopotamia, where the lamb was associated with the mother goddess, Ninhursag. It was also said that the lamb symbolized Duttur, the mother of Dumuzi, who was an important god of milk, shepherding, and the netherworld. In ancient Egyptian culture, the deity Khnum, the guardian of the river Nile, was portrayed as a ram-headed man. In Christianity, sheep are associated with goodness and purity. Jesus was given the title "lamb of God," as the lamb was often used in sacrificial rites, dying so that others could live.

SKUNK

REPUTATION • SELF-LOVE • RESPECT AND HONOR • BOUNDARIES • POSTURE AND COMPOSURE • POSITIVE ATTENTION • SEXUAL ENERGY

WHEN TO WORK WITH ME:

When you want respect, when you want to cultivate self-love, when you want to heighten sexual relationships, when you need to draw clear boundaries, when you want to insulate yourself from criticism and judgments

ENERGY MEDICINE:

As you embody your true power and gifts, call upon me to attract those who are of similar vibration and to create a healthy boundary between you and those who aren't able to respect or understand the love and medicine you bring.

I demonstrate the power of posture. Do you carry yourself with divine self-respect? Call on my medicine to help you carry yourself with confidence and self-esteem. Remember, you have the power to influence how others see you.

Is it time for you to stand up for yourself? Work with me to peacefully and powerfully convey your stance and perspective. You deserve respect.

When I show up, I foretell of experiencing strong attraction. Call upon me to strengthen a healthy intimate relationship with you and your partner.

If you tend to be overly defensive in an attempt to protect your heart, work with me to reveal whether the boundary you are setting is really protecting you, or whether it's preventing you from having deep experiences and relationships.

POWER PRACTICE:

Skunk embodies self-love, honor, and respect. Skunks release their spray to warn potential predators and set very clear boundaries, giving it a respected and strong reputation in the animal kingdom. For this practice, get out your journal and pen and either sit in nature or in a quiet, private space in your home. Sit tall, with a straight spine, and connect with your breath and heart. Now call on skunk energy and divide the paper into three columns. In the first column, list any people in your life who overstep healthy boundaries with you. Is there anyone invasive or pushy in your life? Someone who asks too much of you? Someone who infringes on your emotional well-being? In the second column, write down any possible reasons for their behavior toward you. You are not excusing the behavior but rather attempting to see what fears or unresolved issues within the other person may be fueling their behavior. Finally, in the third column, list what you need to healthily communicate in order to establish clearer boundaries. For example, if someone is repeatedly bringing up a topic you are not comfortable discussing with them, plan to have a conversation where—without anger or drama—you let them know that the subject is now off-limits. Commit to holding these boundaries. If they overstep the boundaries, your next step may be to let them know your communication will end if the topic is brought up again. When your list is complete, ask skunk to stay with you as you practice self-love and self-respect. Setting healthy boundaries will get easier with practice.

SLOTH

COVERT • OMNISCIENT • ENERGY RESERVE • PROTECTING THE UNDERDOG • COMPASSION • METHODICAL

WHEN TO WORK WITH ME:

When you want to stop being judgmental, when you want to be more open-minded, when you need to rest in order to keep going, when you want to be present and enjoy life, when you need to be methodical

ENERGY MEDICINE:

Have you given someone a fair chance, or did you jump to a conclusion or judgment? Aim to be as compassionate as possible right now and see things from the other's perspective.

I teach of honoring differences. Just because someone lives or works differently than you does not make their way negative or "bad."

I remind you to conserve your energy so that you can stay the course. If you are on the verge of giving up on something, ask yourself whether a temporary break to restore your energy could be all you need to keep going.

Are you able to be present and truly enjoy the journey of life? Or are you always striving for and looking to what is next? I teach of being at one with the glory of the present moment.

I remind you of the power of moving through life in a very conscious, methodical way. Take time to tune in to the wisdoms of the Earth and nature overall to nourish and inspire you.

I empower you to not waste energy on things that are not important and to not get stuck in any feeling or process. My medicine is steadiness and flow.

POWER PRACTICE:

Sloths live in harmony with trees; they derive their nourishment, get their rest, and make their homes in trees. They even give birth in trees. For this practice, you will connect directly with a tree in your backyard, your neighborhood, or in a local park. Give yourself at least 10 minutes with the tree, and commit to being completely present in this moment. Sit or stand beneath the tree and gently observe all its parts, beginning at the base. Move your attention up the tree slowly and intentionally, like a sloth. Notice how the tree connects with the earth beneath it. Follow each branch. Notice the movement of the leaves. Bring your gaze all the way to the treetop. Before you leave, touch the bark with your hands and softly thank the tree for all that it provides.

SNAIL

SPIRITUAL EVOLUTION • PATH OF LEAST RESISTANCE • CONSCIOUS AWARENESS • PACE • INTIMACY • EXPANSION

WHEN TO WORK WITH ME:

When you want to find a way to work that is not too fast or stressful, when you want to break out of your comfort zone, when you want to choose the easiest path, when you want to reconsider the pace of a relationship

ENERGY MEDICINE:

My ability to produce my own slime as I move allows me to traverse all landscapes with the greatest ease, including rising up vertically without falling off. Call on me to illuminate the path of least resistance.

Remember that faster is not always better. Call upon me when you need to slow the pace of something or feel more ease as you go.

I remind you to take the time to celebrate your victories, big and small. Enjoy the process of working toward your ultimate goal.

Have you fallen into patterns of habit and familiarity? My medicine will help you change things up and invite new, exciting experiences into your life.

Take a deeper look at the projects you're working on, the relationships you have, and the leisure activities you engage in. Are they truly nurturing and uplifting your soul?

POWER PRACTICE:

One of snail's greatest teachings is reminding us of the rewards that come with slowing things down within a relationship. This practice is a simple yet powerful inquiry into the pace of intimacy in your life. Have you observed that you rush into physical interactions quickly, sometimes with less than satisfying results? Are you going through the motions, rather than making sure you're getting what you want? And if you're in a healthy, romantic partnership, when was the last time you shared slow, sensual moments with your partner or took time to tune in more deeply to your own sensual energy? Slowing things down with a partner or yourself can open up new, higher-oscillating energies that will greatly enhance your life.

SHELL SYMBOLISM

Snails have a spiral-shaped shell, which ancient Egyptians associated with the idea of expansion and evolution. According to renowned psychologist Carl Jung, the spiral symbolizes the unconscious, the inward journey, and the underworld.

SNAKE

TRANSCENDENCE • TRANSMUTATION • SHEDDING THE OLD • SEXUAL FIRE • LIFE FORCE • CREATIVITY

WHEN TO WORK WITH ME:

When you are ready to let go of what no longer serves you, when you want to set yourself free, when you are ready to awaken your true spiritual life force from within, when you want to align with your divine sexual and creative powers

ENERGY MEDICINE:

I am here to assist you in shedding your old skin—it is time to transmute and be reborn.

I evoke sensuality, sexual energy, fertility. My medicine makes you feel alive. If you are feeling my call, your creative forces are awakening. What creation are you ready to give birth to?

Call upon me to assist in raising your kundalini energy—the life force that leads to spiritual awakening. I help you clear each chakra so that you can connect to the spiritual plane.

I can teach you how to see into the heart of others; work with me to reveal sacred truths.

When I appear, pay closer attention to the guidance and whispers of your higher self. I am also a sign that your intuition is strengthening.

POWER PRACTICE:

In this practice, you'll work with snake to shed and release anything you're ready to leave behind. Find a quiet, comfortable place to lie. Close your eyes and visualize yourself as a snake slithering along the earth. Consider what you're ready to release in your life. Is something holding you back or stifling your creativity? Are you carrying something that you're ready to let go of? This is your old skin, ready to be shed. Now feel your snake skin begin to release from your body as you slide forward. Glance behind you and see the old skin, no longer part of you. Acknowledge what you're shedding and then continue moving forward.

Open your eyes and move your limbs to return to your body. Snake is calling upon you to connect with your new energy and activate it through movement. Turn on a song that makes you feel something powerful and give yourself *complete* freedom to let your body move. Dance, stretch, roll on the ground, whatever feels right. As you are moving, call snake's potent life force to fill your body with fresh energy. When you feel the practice is complete, thank snake for helping you release the old and embrace the new.

A SYMBOL OF ETERNITY

The ouroboros, a circular image of a serpent with its tail in its mouth, is a symbol of eternity and continuous renewal. The symbol dates back to ancient Egypt and later appeared in Greek and Druid art and jewelry.

"I was ten years old when Mamba, the snake, blessed me with my first shamanic initiation. It was an overcast morning in the wild eastern part of South Africa known as the 'bush-veld.' I was hunting impala with my father to provide meat for the people of the village, and we had crawled up the side of a termite mound to position ourselves for a shot.

"Together, my father and I lay against the mound in the thick grass and peered over the top at the impala grazing below us. That's when I felt death slipping across my legs. I looked down in horror and saw the gunmetal, scaled skin of the black mamba. Its head was shaped like a coffin, and it wore a deadly smile across its face. Mambas are widely considered to be the deadliest snake on earth. One bite would rapidly send me to the other side of the veil.

"Though my mind screamed with fear, my reaction came from a deeper, wilder, more instinctual place, and I knew to stay extremely still. 'Dad, there is a mamba on me. DON'T MOVE!' We lay motionless for a few minutes while the mamba slid over my legs with the slow intensity of a drill sergeant inspecting the barracks. Blood dripped out of my father's mouth as he bit his cheek to hold his nerve. Then, the mamba turned and slowly made its way back down into a hole in the termite mound.

"I didn't know it at the time, but my medicine journey had begun. Mamba had taught me the way of opposites that a shaman must learn. To be still when others would panic. To balance on the thin line between life and death like a fearless acrobat. Mamba showed me what it was like to carry yourself with intensity and respect. That day, the snake taught me that I can choose my reaction and that some terrifying things mean us no harm if we can allow them their way."

—Boyd Varty

STORYTELLER AND LION TRACKER, LONDOLOZI GAME RESERVE, SOUTH AFRICA

**NEW LIFE WEAVER • MAGIC • ACTIVATION • CREATION •
ENDING STIGMA • CREATIVE LIFE FORCE**

WHEN TO WORK WITH ME:

When embarking on a new phase of life, when you desire harmony, when you want to activate more magic in your life, when you want to transcend fear, when you want to approach things with curiosity, when you're ready to move forward with intention

ENERGY MEDICINE:

I am the weaver of new life. I activate new worlds and new opportunities.

Work with me to have trust in a much more expanded vision of your life. I can teach you about transcending from fear to reverence, to shift from labeling and misjudging to openheartedness and curiosity.

I ask you to tune in to your surroundings and to ask yourself these questions: "What wisdoms are speaking to me, ready to empower me?" Do you trust that you have the energy and intelligence inside of you, right now, to manifest your grandest visions?" It's time to weave your web.

I represent creative life force. I help you think about the unique ways you can express your teachings and gifts and what unexpected or new ways of delivering your energetic medicines you can offer the world. What does your unique web of magic look and feel like?

I urge you to access your inner light and divine trust in self and the Universe, and to move forward by feeling your way through. Trust and step, trust and step.

I work with you and other members of your soul family to bring you together to weave more cocreative magic and light for this world in your relationships. When wanting to call upon a harmonious partnership, collaboration, or romantic relationship, ask me for my blessings and guidance during meditation.

POWER PRACTICE:

Gather a piece of paper and a pen, and find a quiet place to sit. Keep your back straight and place the bottoms of your feet on the floor, then connect to your breath, release your shoulders from your ears, and loosen your jaw. Close your eyes and sit this way for several minutes. When you sense it's time to open your eyes, do so. On the piece of paper, begin drawing your own web. In the middle of the page, draw a small circle and write your name inside. Then, draw a larger circle around the first circle, and connect the two circles with words that represent the things you want to experience in your spiritual life. Then, draw a third circle, and connect the third and second circles with words that represent the positive things you want to activate in your relationships. Finally, draw a fourth circle, and connect the fourth and third circles with words related to the things you want to manifest in your work. Now take a look at your web and see all the interconnected experiences, relationships, and feelings. Know that each layer and connection is working together to create harmony in your life.

SPIDER SILK

The spider is the only animal on the planet that builds webs. Spider silk, the material used to build webs, is made of liquid proteins that become solid when they leave the spider's body. Spider silk is stronger by weight than steel, yet elastic enough to stretch to as much as five times its length before breaking.

"Spider came in as I was in the beginning activations of the most powerful and joyous time of my life. I had just shifted from being close friends to a sacred, romantic partnership with my partner. As we began taking steps to first share our love with the world, spider revealed over and over to me, communicating its blessing of our union and urging us to keep moving forward in weaving our new life of magic together. Now knowing spider is one of our main totems as a couple, I'm excited to walk forward in our joy and trust in one another, the Universe, and ourselves, and to continuously be open to seeing new ways we can share, teach, and express our unique magic with the world."

—Alyson Charles

SQUIRREL

PREPAREDNESS • ACTION • WORK AND PLAY BALANCE • DIVINE TIMING • TRUST • SOLUTIONS

WHEN TO WORK WITH ME:

When you need more play in your life, when you want the security of ample resources, when you want to declutter, when you want to trust the cycles of movement and rest, when you want confidence to take action

ENERGY MEDICINE:

I teach the importance of preparing and securing proper bounty to best support you in the future. Work with me to keep an abundant supply of what you feel is most important, but don't hoard that which you do not truly need.

I bring forth the medicine of play. Working toward your goals is vital, but remember that lightheartedness and adventure will recharge you and help you avoid burnout.

Are you scurrying frantically in lots of different directions with no clear plan? Take a breather, spend some time engaging in play, and come back with clarity. Choose one thing to focus on first.

Do not push your body, energy, or spirit when you truly feel called to rest. Trust your natural cycles and know that rest will fuel you so that you can move forward with restored energy.

Learning through stepping forward and taking action is what I recommend. Don't stifle yourself or procrastinate due to fear.

My main medicine is a "no worry mind." I show you how to effortlessly pivot to try new avenues and solutions when one path doesn't seem to be working. Know you'll find your way.

POWER PRACTICE:

You've likely heard the phrase "bright-eyed and bushy-tailed," inspired by squirrel's appearance. Close your eyes and tune in to that image, seeing squirrel's lively eyes and full tail as it scampers through a forest. Next, think about one thing in your life you would like to have a better solution for. When you're clear on what that thing is, call bright squirrel in to work with you. Say, "Beautiful squirrel, I invite you to reveal a solution to ____. I ask that you show me this solution now." Ask as many times as you need, and in between asking, sit calmly with your eyes closed, connected with your breath, simply allowing an answer to be revealed. Squirrel may even enter into your mind's eye and hand you an acorn or a nut that holds the solution inside. If this happens, put the acorn or nut up to your ear and listen for what it has to share. After you get an answer, thank your squirrel friend and follow through. That part is up to you.

UNIQUE PATH • INTUITION • EXPANSION • ALCHEMY •
INFINITE NATURE • EMOTIONAL SENSITIVITY •
SACRED PARTNERSHIP • GENEROSITY

WHEN TO WORK WITH ME:

When you want to experience infinite love, when you're in need of clarity, when you're ready to embrace your unique soul purpose, when you want to stabilize your emotions, when you want to forge ahead regardless of what others say, when you want to be more generous

ENERGY MEDICINE:

My medicine helps you follow your intuition, no matter how strange it may seem (especially to others).

Could you be better about casting judgments on others? Remember how important it is for you to uniquely be you without fear of judgment. Aim to give others the same respect.

Remember that you will always prevail if you are moving with the current of personal truth, integrity, and your unique Earth mission. When you fully step into your unique power, you act from a place of knowing you are always blessed, guided, and protected.

I remind you that you are fully equipped with very powerful abilities to sense all: what to do, how you feel, what is best for you, and so on. Trust your innate knowing.

Be honest with yourself if your desire to have things go the way you want or have someone like you in a certain way is leading you to exude manipulative behaviors. Keep this in check.

When was the last time you lent a hand to help or empower another? I call on you to be generous with your energy and time.

POWER PRACTICE:

Sacred starfish represents unique power and divine, infinite love, and it relies only on the sense of touch to navigate. You will do a unique meditation centered around these beautiful traits. Gather a blindfold and earplugs or headphones (something to cover your eyes and ears) and sit in a quiet, private, comfortable space in your home. Once you cover your eyes and ears, call starfish forward to be your guide in this meditation. Begin to connect with your breath and heart center. Now, begin to move your hands over your body. Notice how your skin, joints, bones, and muscles feel. Notice the quality of the pressure of your hands as you send infinite love to your body. You can also do this practice with a romantic partner, sitting across from one another and respectfully touching each other's sacred bodies as you send infinite love to one another. Enjoy this exploration for as long as you need. Remove the blindfold and earplugs, and thank starfish for sharing this practice with you.

STINGRAY

CALM • DIVINE TINGLES (OR COMMUNICATION) • EASY NAVIGATION • NONCONFRONTATION • DEEP THOUGHTS

WHEN TO WORK WITH ME:

When you want time to yourself, when you need a break, when you want to avoid drama or conflict, when you want to get to the root of healing emotional patterns, when you want support in knowing how to pick and choose battles, when you do not want to react from emotions

ENERGY MEDICINE:

If you feel drawn to me, you likely value alone time but are always up for a deep, thought-provoking conversation.

I bring an air of mystery with me, often surprising others when I feel inspired to passionately express. Call on me to evoke your creative ideas and fun ways to bring them to life.

Choosing your battles is one of my main medicine teachings. If things feel heated or on the verge of battle, take a long pause before deciding how to best proceed. How can you address the issue without anger or confrontation? Approaching things with calm reason will have more impact.

My medicine is electric. Have you ever experienced a tingling or an electrical sensation on your skin? Pay attention. These divine tingles are likely trying to signal something. What messages are coming through?

I am your reminder to pay attention if a repeated challenging emotion surfaces. Our emotions are our teachers, and continually ignoring an emotional message does not allow for full transformation or healing.

POWER PRACTICE:

Stingray represents avoiding unnecessary drama and conflict. In this practice, you'll use breathwork to cultivate calm energy so that you can deal with things in a cool, levelheaded manner. Sit tall in a comfortable chair with your feet flat on the ground. Rest the palms of your hands on the tops of your thighs. Close your eyes and for the next 2 minutes, practice what is known as "box breathing." Inhale through your nose for 4 seconds, then hold the breath for 4 seconds, then exhale through your nose for 4 seconds, then hold the breath for 4 seconds. Repeat this sequence for 2 minutes. Once this is complete, you should feel calmer and more grounded. Do this practice any time you feel reactive or need to calm down before speaking.

STORK

BIRTHING PROCESS • CHILDREN AND FAMILY • HOMELIFE •
INNER CHILD • RENEWAL • ROOTS • ICONIC • SOUL • FERTILITY

WHEN TO WORK WITH ME:

When you want to heal childhood or ancestral wounds, when you want to birth something new, when you want to have healthy roots and a stable home, when you want to connect with other realms, when you're ready to have good fortune and prosperity

ENERGY MEDICINE:

I herald a time of new opportunity or new birth for you. I am a fiercely loving protector; my medicine will nourish and nurture.

I remind you of the importance of healing your inner child and ancestral roots. This essential work creates new possibilities for your lineage while moving forward.

I represent a time of renewal for you and your life. Take time to disrupt old patterns to allow for an opening in these rich winds of change.

I come bearing news of increasing good fortune. Welcome these feelings of comfort, support, and abundance. You are deserving.

I bring forward the ability to activate warrior goddess energy. Call upon me to activate this sacred power.

If you want to activate your ability to connect with unseen realms, this is one of my greatest gifts. Work with me to support you in this sacred travel.

POWER PRACTICE:

Stork has a reputation of delivering new life, and in this practice, you will call on stork to help you provide new energy to someone you know. Close your eyes and inquire within: "Whom can I support today in a loving way? How can I most positively impact this person's life?" Consider what you can give to someone that would powerfully provide them with hope, support, and abundance. Whatever answers are revealed, act on them. By embodying stork, you can provide people with what they need on the soul level, which in turn will help both you and them feel connected, worthy, and loved.

STORKS AND NEWBORNS

The symbolism of storks delivering babies can be traced back more than 600 years to early practices of paganism in medieval times. Many couples would get married during the summer solstice because they associated summer with fertility. Around this same time of year, storks would begin their once-a-year migration from Europe to Africa. Nine months later would coincide with the storks returning to have their babies, thus their association with "delivering" the babies and representing new life.

SWAN

ARTS AND POETRY • SACRED LOVE • GRACE • SELF-ESTEEM • REGAL BEAUTY • SPIRITUAL REALIZATION • WEALTH

WHEN TO WORK WITH ME:

When you want a sacred partnership, when you are ready for more wealth, when you want to access your intuitive powers, when you want to embody more grace and beauty, when you want to be more comfortable in a group

ENERGY MEDICINE:

My regal, graceful presence inspires art, poetry, and sacred love.

My powerful medicine reminds you that you are most effective when you follow your intuition. I show you that recognizing your inner beauty takes you to new realms and activates your gifts within that can only be born when you gain a deeper connection to your self-worth.

I am here to share that accepting the healing and transformation that is now happening in your life will allow for more ease. Surrender.

I can help you be comfortable in large groups and crowds, while being assured your unique essence and beauty can still shine.

My wings hold wisdom from Great Spirit, and I assist you in spiritual realization.

POWER PRACTICE:

In this practice, you'll invite swan's powerful medicine into your life through a creative endeavor. Take an hour to engage in an artistic exercise. This could be writing poetry, painting a picture, composing a song, or sculpting something out of clay. Ask swan to be with you as you explore your artistic side. As you go through this practice, hold the image of swan in your mind and take pride in your work, carrying yourself with dignity and grace. Trust in the process. You are expressing your unique, beautiful essence in the form of artwork.

A SYMBOL OF ART, MUSIC, AND POETRY

In Greek mythology, the swan was closely associated with the Muses, poetry, music, and the mystery of high verse. In one Greek myth, Orpheus, a mortal with superhuman musical skills and the son of Calliope, the patron of epic poetry, is torn to pieces by Ciconian women angered that he didn't worship their god. After his death, Orpheus was reborn as a swan.

TICK

FACING FEARS • HEIGHTENED AWARENESS • DISCOMFORT •
ANCIENT CONSCIOUSNESS • HEALING TRAUMA

WHEN TO WORK WITH ME:

When you want to practice nonattachment, when you want to embody your full power, when you want to transcend your fears, when you don't want to ignore what's holding you back anymore, when you want to alchemize and heal trauma

ENERGY MEDICINE:

My medicine can be very confrontational. I can instantly take you to places and depths within yourself that you haven't explored in a long time. Trust your ability to navigate this.

Call on me to face the fears you've been avoiding. When fear presents, do you spin out into terrified thoughts? My medicine will help you stay centered so that you can understand the fear and eventually access a higher and more resolute state of being.

I share an offering of the remembrance that you cannot embody your full power without first doing shadow work. By facing aspects of yourself or your life that you'd rather ignore because they are too terrifying or shameful, you actually empower and free yourself.

Is someone or something invading your energy? Is there any attachment in your life that you need to disengage from? Call on me to aid in this process.

I remind you that even anguishing moments can turn out to be miraculous gifts.

POWER PRACTICE:

While this creature may not be the prettiest or most appealing power animal, tick reminds us to respect that all beings have incredibly important messages and teachings, no matter their outward appearance. In fact, many life experiences are similar in that they may initially present as scary, unpleasant, or dark but end up revealing untapped power within us or opportunities to improve our lives. In this practice, you will work with tick to face discomfort in order to bring forth your greatest self. To begin, sit in a quiet, private space with your journal and pen. Close your eyes, connect with your heart and breath, and call tick forward to be your guide. Ask yourself, "When I'm scared or uncomfortable, what distractions do I go to?" Ask it as many times as you need, allow all answers to be revealed, and log them in your journal. Then, ask yourself, "Next time I am filled with fear, how can I stay present? What tools do I have to remain calm and centered as I face discomfort?" Record your answers in your journal. Thank yourself and tick for being willing to bring forward this potent and vital information that allows for deepest transformation.

Note: If you need guidance in processing or healing from any of the information presented, be sure to reach out to a trusted therapist or healer. This kind of deep emotional work requires support.

"'May you feel every tick' is a phrase my wife and I say each spring as the last snows melt in New England. Walking through the woods or fields between the last snow and the first inevitably leaves us searching our bodies for ticks. Finding a dozen isn't unusual.

"In centuries past, this part of the world was home to charismatic predatory megafauna, like wolves and mountain lions. After wanton human extirpation tamed this landscape, people didn't need to pay attention anymore and a kind of blunted awareness took hold. That was, until the rise of the ticks.

"While we're inspired by the elegance of the puma or the nobility of the wolf pack, the uncomely tick is often—and easily—overlooked. And that's just how they prefer it, going unseen and unfelt as they quest after a quiet, cozy piece of flesh on which to feed.

"There's wisdom to be gained from these unpleasant little creatures: sensitivity and constant awareness. We've learned that we must listen to even the faintest signal from our bodies that something's crawling on our skin. Ticks are masters of covert operations—you scarcely notice their presence. We've become adept at detecting even the subtlest sensations of their eight little legs, but we don't rely on feel alone. We use our vision as well. Twice daily, naked under bright light, we examine ourselves in the mirror. Every nook, anywhere a tick might hide. No freckle goes unexamined, no mole unscrutinized. This practice has deepened our comfort with our bodies and made us like auto-physicians, conducting daily health exams upon ourselves. We've become medically vigilant.

"Ticks have made us better people. More aware, more conscientious, more awake. Ticks are more than antagonists. They are our teachers too, and for that, we thank them."

—Daniel Vitalis

REGISTERED MAINE GUIDE
AND HOST OF *WILDFED*

TIGER

NOCTURNAL POWER • WATER • ENERGETIC BURSTS • TOUCH • LEADERSHIP • DETERMINATION • PASSION • SELFISHNESS • NEW ADVENTURE

WHEN TO WORK WITH ME:

When you want to awaken sensuality and passion, when you want to grow stronger with each lesson in life, when you want strong focus, when you're ready for new adventures, when you need energy, when you want to be a great leader

ENERGY MEDICINE:

Healing energy is one of my strongest attributes. When I present in your life, your journey may be filled with some confrontational teachings. But these teachings all bring illumination, allowing you to become fully embodied.

I represent the power of touch and sensuality. Does your body need touch? Check in with yourself to see how long it's been since you've gotten a hug, a massage, or had a loving experience with a partner. Human touch is revitalizing and sustaining.

I bring forward a time of reinvigorated passion. Be aware of new adventures or opportunities presenting. Seize them.

Observe whether you've been having any selfish tendencies lately. Is there someone you can be more gracious, compassionate, and generous toward?

I activate an unparalleled ability to awaken leadership abilities and ensure success. Work with me to lead with confidence, passion, and clarity.

POWER PRACTICE:

Tiger is known for connecting deeply with the element of water and energies of the night, so this practice will involve those essences. This evening, ask yourself which of the following tiger power animal traits speak the most to you right now: leadership, determination, or a renewed passion for life. Pick one to activate in this practice.

When it's dark, bring a bowl of water outside with you to leave under the energy of the moon and call upon tiger to join you in this ritual. Spend a few moments speaking to the water, asking that it be infused with blessings for the attribute you've selected. Connect with the water with your fingers or hands. You can place another sacred item, like a crystal, stone, leaf, flower, stick, or feather, in the water as an offering to this blessing and to tiger. Next, begin to imagine the way it will feel to experience the attribute you've chosen—leadership, determination, or a renewed passion for life—while looking into the water. When the process is complete, thank the water and tiger and ask the moon to bless all of your intentions and the water overnight. The next morning, when you return to the water, use your intuition to determine what you want to do with the water—drink it, add it to a bath, keep it on your altar, or discard it. Let your heart guide you.

YEAR OF THE TIGER

In ancient Chinese astrology, in a year of the tiger, people set in motion projects, visions, or goals that may not be completed for many years or even generations. The tiger represents setting strong foundations and being a kind of philosopher who is not overwhelmed by the conditions of the moment, but mindful of generations yet to come.

"The tiger is the most respected animal in our community. When we are looking to a being that is sweet and kind and also moves forward and takes action, we look to the tiger. When babies are born, the elders know whether that baby has special spiritual gifts. For the newborns who do, their doula brings the liquid of a special plant to help activate the spirit by placing it in their nose. They know that when someone carries this special gift, they have to be strong and cannot get sick, so this plant protects them from any illnesses. From a very young age, these children are also being watched by the elders for their spiritual gifts, checking in to make sure they're guided, following their commitment to their gift, and exhibiting good behavior. It's during this time that the child is also introduced to the tobacco plant and the liquid of the tobacco. They put the liquid up their nose and also blow the tobacco smoke into the crown of their head, as this is where they receive all their wisdom. For 25 years, the people carrying the gifts continue preparing and using the tobacco plant, which gives them the strength needed to move through the waters and mountains and to be able to activate themselves. They are trained to release fear because it can get in the way of wisdom. They are taught that by being courageous, they receive access to eternal wisdom.

"When the gifted person is initiated, they're able to receive the wisdom of nature and those around them and can access the wisdom of the medicinal properties of plants. The ultimate granter of all this sacred wisdom is the tiger. In order to access the spirit world, they connect with the tiger, ancestors, and elders who have guided their way. Then, when they are fifty-five or sixty years old, and have followed their mission and path, they can choose to live their life as a tiger or a human. They can shape-shift back and forth, but it is a matter of knowing when they need human food and when they need animal spirit food.

"Later, when the person is old and dies, they no longer shape-shift and their spirit transforms into the tiger. This is the metamorphosis in our culture. Only the chosen ones can shape-shift. It takes a lot of practice and training. My grandmother, who is ninety-eight years old, is a shape-shifter with the tiger. My godmother was too. Shape-shifters can be men or women and in different Amazonian cultures, they can shift into different animals or plants, but in our community it is the tiger."

—Juan Andi Vargas

THE TIGER, SPIRITUAL GUIDE FROM THE KICHWAS NATION OF THE AMAZON

TURTLE

GROUNDING • PROTECTION • ANCIENT WISDOM • PERSISTENCE • PRESENCE • FAITH • ABUNDANCE • FERTILITY

WHEN TO WORK WITH ME:

When you need to feel protected, when you want to feel more grounded, when you want to connect with the Earth, when you're ready to tune in to ancient wisdom, when you need endurance, when you want to invite abundance and fertility

ENERGY MEDICINE:

Call to me when you need to get grounded, connect with your body more, and connect with Great Mother Earth.

I bring forth energies of fertility and abundance and help you remember to enjoy the journey, to be present.

Work with me when you want to be re-centered in the knowingness that you are exactly where you need to be at this time. Be confident in your path and your timing. One step at a time, one step at a time—that's all you need to get you there.

Use my shell by envisioning it around you as a protective barrier, shielding you from negativity, jealousy, resentment, or anything lower realm.

Work with me when you need an extra dose of persistence and endurance, or a reminder not to be afraid to ask for help.

I help you surrender into the deep wisdom that lives within you. Do not fight what is trying to emerge from you at this time.

POWER PRACTICE:

This practice is designed for when you have absorbed other people's negative energies, energies that are not yours to carry and not serving your highest good. It is also useful when you are going into a situation or conversation where you would like a protective force. For this practice, find a place to sit comfortably in a brief meditation. Close your eyes and visualize the shell of turtle surrounding you, large enough to cover your body. Feel the medicine of the turtle shell protecting you from anything not serving your highest good. Imagine the shell illuminating, creating a thick, golden-white aura all around you. Watch this light getting brighter and brighter, completely enveloping you as you say: "I am held and fully protected by the loving energies of turtle. Thank you for taking care of me and always guiding me home."

ANCIENT AND OLD

Turtles are an ancient species, dating back to the time of dinosaurs, more than 200 million years ago. Their life span can also be very long. It's believed that some sea turtles may be 400 to 500 years old. All turtles are completely attached to their shells. The shells do not come off, and they grow as the turtle grows.

VULTURE

PURIFIER • SEER • ENERGY PRESERVATION • LIFE FROM DEATH • FRIENDSHIP AND COMMUNITY

WHEN TO WORK WITH ME:

When you want to be in a healthy community, when you want more kindness in your life, when you want to be purified, when you want to open abilities to read auras, when you want to open your clairvoyant gifts, when you don't want to feel lost or alone anymore, when you want to rise from hard times better than ever

ENERGY MEDICINE:

I share the ability to maintain your energy, even when encountering challenging people or experiences.

My energy ushers lost or disconnected souls back home to themselves. If this is you, call upon me for my powerful support.

One of my greatest medicines is being able to be nourished from darkness or death. That is to say, I have the ability to experience a hard time or loss and turn it into positive fuel, every time.

I empower your ability to become prophetic or incredibly clairvoyant, awakening your gift to access different planes and realms and return to your body with information.

Call upon me if you want to open your ability to see and read people's auras and also when working with different goddesses, like Sekhmet, Kali, Nekhbet, or Mut.

I embody and remind you of the power of friendship, community, and kindness. These attributes, along with my very specific shamanic medicine around cleansing and renewing, support my powers in being a great divine purifier. This allows others to be deeply, positively changed simply by being in my presence.

POWER PRACTICE:

Vulture is an incredibly powerful and sacred creature that can deeply impact your life when you're in its presence. In this practice, you'll embody vulture's power to change the energy of a space. Reflect now for a moment on this question: "When I walk into a room full of people, what medicine (energy, essences, emotions) do I transmit simply by being there?" Be very honest with yourself. Perhaps you bring calm energy, or perhaps you must acknowledge that you bring anxiety into a space. Then ask yourself, "What medicine do I ideally want to transmit to other people, simply by being in the room?" Consider how you can lift others in a healthy way, using your unique energy. How will you hold your body? What will you say? How will you listen? Aim to be a great purifier of a space in a positive manner, remembering that if you embody compassion, love, and other uplifting essences, that is what will be most reflected back to you. Refer to this vulture energy practice any time you are around other people and notice how it improves the quality of your relationships, your sense of self, and the mood of your friends and loved ones.

A SYMBOL OF NEW LIFE AND FERTILITY

Ancient Mayans revered the vulture for its ability to clean and renew the Earth by transforming death into new life. This deeply powerful purification skill is also seen in the ancient Egyptian belief that all vultures are female, which happens through a process called *parthenogenesis*—reproduction without any needed fertilization from a male. This gave vultures the ultimate symbolism of purity and fertility.

Fire Vulture
dance
on my terrestrial bones
What have I to offer you?
at this altar of flesh?
Give me your eyes
she says
so you may seem to
Devour
with me
and all will Be

—Abbey Gibb
DIVINE MESSAGING MENTOR

WALRUS

KNOWLEDGE • RE-PRIORITIZATION • PURPOSE • FAMILY LOVE • SOCIABILITY • AFFECTION

WHEN TO WORK WITH ME:

When you want to gain deeper knowledge, when you need to embody parental love, when you need affection, when you want to be more sociable, when you want to host a gathering, when you want to see more beauty in the world

ENERGY MEDICINE:

I represent strong medicine of nourishing and nurturing loved ones. This is an area of life you have the ability to excel in, so allow yourself to grow in this way and, in turn, help others grow too.

When was the last time you were social or initiated a gathering? Think about who it would be great to form community with and how that might support you.

If I resonate deeply with you, you are someone who sees and appreciates the beauty in all. You are secure in yourself, which allows you to celebrate the beauty in others.

I am present when a time of deepening one's wisdom and knowledge is at hand. Take time now to fully understand the new project, information, or collaboration. When you have all the knowledge you need, proceed fully equipped.

Ask yourself where you can receive or share a healthy dose of affection today.

POWER PRACTICE:

Walrus is known for being nonaggressive despite its massive size and intimidating tusks. For this practice, meditate on walrus's appearance and demeanor, then close your eyes and connect with your breath and heart. Once this connection is established, ask yourself whether there are any areas or relationships in your life (including the relationship you have with yourself) where a deeper sense of calm and greater affection can occur. If something surfaces, ask walrus to work with you in developing a more positive attitude toward this person or situation.

WHALE

TELEPATHY • ANCIENT RECORD KEEPER • COMMUNICATION • SONG • POWER • REGENERATION • RELEASE • UPLEVELING

WHEN TO WORK WITH ME:

When you want to tap into more spiritual energies, when you want to work with sound and song, when you want a boost in life, when you need to communicate better, when you want to stay in your power, when you want to connect to Great Mother Earth

ENERGY MEDICINE:

When I present in life, it signifies a period of upleveling or growth. I am here to provide whatever push, nudge, or support is needed to take you higher.

Is there a conversation that needs to be had? I embody great medicine of ancient sound and communication. Call upon me to guide you in the next steps.

I further activate your spiritual path, especially the ability to transmit messages via song or thought. Work with me to awaken these gifts in you.

What creativity or emotion needs to be expressed through you? If you are suppressing an energy that deeply needs to move or liberate, you have to be honest with yourself and give it freedom.

I possess much ancient wisdom and records, especially pertaining to Great Mother Earth. Work with me to heal ancestral or lineage traumas and to tap into collective human consciousness.

I lovingly and powerfully bring you the awareness that there is much more happening in your life than what your human eyes can see. Remember your ancient ways, remember the unseen realms, remember you are here to awaken from illusion and limitation. Let me be your guide.

POWER PRACTICE:

You will work with three of whale's main medicines for this practice: curiosity, song, and spiritual access. Tune in first to whale—its size, power, and energy as an ancient record keeper for Great Mother Earth. Now, call upon whale to work with you in this ritual. If you have any sort of instrument at home, whether it's a drum, rattle, or guitar, gather it now. Or you can simply sing. Let yourself be as fluid and at one with the Universe as the ocean water. With whale as your guide, invite it into your heart and let yourself be carried into making the sounds that want to come out. Stay with this process and let yourself be free. If at any point you wish to close your eyes, stay in your heart, create a repetitive beat, or allow any insights or spiritual energies to make their way to you, do so. Whether you feel totally at home with this practice or wildly uncomfortable, I invite you to do it as often as possible and keep opening yourself to the spiritual wisdoms your soul wants to access.

MYSTERIOUS SONG

Humpback whales are known for their haunting songs. Scientists have studied their communications, which include howls, moans, whispers, and other complex noises that sometimes last for hours. We know humpbacks use echolocation—making noise and listening for the reflected sound—to explore their surroundings using high-pitched sounds and clicks. But the purpose of their songs is still a mystery.

"Whales have played a powerful role for me since I was a young child, making themselves and their medicines known in many different ways. As I grew older and was trying to get pregnant, I saw a mother and baby whale in front of our home in Malibu. I took that as a sign that my baby was coming, and six months later, I got pregnant. Even more recently, I told two girlfriends that I wanted to take some time off work to recharge my batteries, spend time with my baby, and find inspiration for the next project. I was burnt out. My friend said, 'When I listen to you speak, I picture a whale. Sometimes, whales need to dive deep and stay in silence and solitude. They rest to get reinspired. Then, when they feel ready, they come up and breech. That's their output or productivity and action phase.' Two months later, COVID-19 hit, and while that time was challenging to many, it was my chance to take that pause, rest, and dive deep like the whale.

"Then, just two months after lockdown began, I saw a kayaker paddling next to a couple of whale spouts. I grabbed my camera, hopped on my paddleboard, and paddled along with them for about half a mile [800 m]. The whales kept coming closer and closer to me, which was an incredible feeling. At the end of the encounter, a teenage whale came up right under my board to say hello. He was literally inches away, but he didn't disturb my board. He just came intuitively close and checked me out. As he dove under my board, he flapped his tail as if to say, 'Hello, friend.' It was a magical encounter, blissful.

"Whales remind me that you can be equal parts introvert and extrovert. Sometimes you need solitude and silence to go within and do the deep work. Sometimes you need to come to the surface, be with your friends, release a creative project into the world, and breech in playful contentment."

—Kelly Noonan Gores

WRITER AND DIRECTOR
OF *HEAL* DOCUMENTARY

WOLF

TEACHER • PSYCHIC INSIGHT • SOCIAL BALANCE • FULL MOON • INDEPENDENCE • NEW GUIDANCE • MEDICINE CARRIER • DIVINE CONFIDENCE • RITUAL

WHEN TO WORK WITH ME:

When you want to strike a balance between being independent and social, when you want to be the best teacher you can be, when you want to embody strong family values, when you want to connect to nature, when you need self-confidence, when you want to align with the powers of the moon

ENERGY MEDICINE:

One of my strongest medicines is helping anchor you in total confidence of who you are. From this place there is nothing to prove or persuade.

When was the last time you spent time alone to unlock your consciousness? The healer or teacher within always needs ample time to dive deep and reveal truths.

I remind you of how vital it is to honor one's elders. In our pack, they lead the way and set the pace. How can you better adopt this in your own life?

Are you following projects through to completion, or are you hastily moving from thing to thing, place to place? I teach of leadership through staying the course.

I awaken a renewed sense of life and ritual and share great medicine for your spirit and soul. If you do not have a regular spiritual practice, I remind you of the importance of devotion and ritual.

I remind you that facing your own mortality can help you find true liberation.

POWER PRACTICE:

In this practice, you'll envision wolf's ability to be both communal and independent. Wolves can be one with the pack, embodying deep family values, and they can also thrive as the "lone wolf," in complete freedom on their own. Close your eyes and take a moment to reflect on which state you are currently in: Are you community-driven or independent? Next, ask yourself whether you feel you've been living in a healthy balance between the two, or whether you have leaned too far in one direction. Some of us are predisposed to one or the other, but you can gain unique and valuable teachings both from spending time alone and spending time in community. Alone, you can learn how to rely on yourself and develop self-knowledge. In spending time with others, you make sacred connections and find support. It's important to regularly consider how you're balancing independence and community.

If you have been spending a lot of time alone, ask yourself whether you have any resistance to spending time with others, and if so, where that is coming from? If you have codependent tendencies, consider what fears may be keeping you from spending time on your own. Whatever was revealed in this inner investigation, invite wolf in to assist you if you are ready to be more sure-footed in the direction you've been lacking. To nurture your relationship with wolf medicine, make an offering to wolf every full moon. It can be as simple as placing a sacred object from nature under the moonlight, or doing a brief meditation thanking wolf for its medicine.

LYCANTHROPY

In folklore, the word *lycanthropy* refers to the transformation of human beings into wolves, usually through magical spells. It derives from the name Lycaon, who was a mythological king of ancient Arcadia (what is now southern Greece). According to legend, Zeus visited Lycaon disguised as a mortal, and Lycaon tested Zeus's divinity by presenting him with a dish of human flesh. Outraged by this sacrilegious act, Zeus transformed Lycaon into a wolf.

"The wolf has been a big part of my life in many ways. When I moved to the United States from Argentina as a child, my nickname changed from Flor ('flower' in Spanish) to Flow ('wolf' spelled backward). It is as if the wolf energy stepped into my experience to guard me and support me in finding the Saq' Be' (the sacred path).

"The leader of the wolf pack always walks behind the pack; the elders of the pack are in front, leading the way and setting the pace. I believe that a true leader is one who can inspire and awaken the leadership qualities in those around them. This is a clear example of the role that the alpha wolf, the leader of the pack, takes on by letting everyone step into their role and then observing from the back of the pack to protect.

"The power animal of the wolf reflects what I aspire to be in this lifetime. I let the elders, the wisdom keepers, the guardians of the sacred lands guide our community. As a leader, I support my tribe by creating a playground and experiences to let each individual remember their own leadership and creative expression as a devotion to living in unconditional love.

"The wolf spirit has also shown me a beautiful balance of how I pursue life. My community and my family mean everything to me. My pack gives me a purpose in this life and reminds me of my mission each and every day. I also truly value my time alone; I find so much bliss in the moments of solo journeys. I often travel alone, take myself out to eat alone, and spend hours in my own creative explorations.

"When I am feeling unclear of what steps to take next, connecting with the spirit of the wolf allows me to deepen my connection with my intuition and inner guidance."

—Florencia Fridman

CEREMONIAL CACAO GUIDE
AND EDUCATOR, COFOUNDER
OF CACAO LABORATORY

WORM

DIGGING INTO THE PAST • EMPOWERMENT • ENVIRONMENT • GROUNDED NOURISHMENT • SELF-HEALING • SOUL WORK

WHEN TO WORK WITH ME:

When you want to feel fulfilled, when you want to connect with the Earth, when you want to see what needs to be healed from your past, when you want to improve your environment

ENERGY MEDICINE:

Are there any events from your past that can be healed more fully? I specialize in this work; call upon me to be your guide.

One of my greatest medicines is connecting directly with the majestic and rich healing energies of the soil. Move past any aversions to putting your hands in the dirt and just go for it.

I teach empowerment and fortitude. Know that even if you are experiencing troubling or challenging times, you can always come back stronger and wiser than ever.

This is a reminder that moving more slowly and methodically is not a bad thing. I teach the productive powers of patience. Tending to your path in a nourishing way will bring fulfillment.

When was the last time you pondered your intention for life? Or gave deep consideration to your current relationships or projects? Operating from a place of clarity and intentional energy can move mountains.

Look at your mind, body, and home as gardens to be tended. What needs more water? What weeds need to be pulled? What can you add that will create a happier, more fertile environment?

POWER PRACTICE:

It's time to dig into your past, guided by worm. Find a quiet place to sit with your eyes closed and your hands on the ground (if you're able do this outside, the practice can be enhanced by placing your hands directly on the earth). Connect with your breath and heart, and invite worm to be with you in this practice. Imagine worm burrowing down into the earth, connecting with the soil. As you watch worm work its way into the ground, begin to turn your attention inward and ask yourself, "Is there anything I deem 'dirty' or 'bad' in my past that needs more healing?" Maybe it's a secret, or a sense of guilt, or a regret. Ask the question as many times as necessary. Once you have identified the part of you that needs healing, ask worm, "Sacred worm, what type of work needs to be done to heal this aspect of my history so that I can move forward with my life?" Take note of the messages that reveal themselves. This type of deep, soul-level work can feel scary or confronting, but the liberation and deep healing on the other side can provide the greatest miracles of your life. It is precisely this type of personal, inner work—going deep into your soul, as the earthworm goes into the earth—that allows you to honor and unconditionally love yourself in full.

Note: If you are confronted by any memories or feelings you do not feel comfortable handling on your own, you can work with a trusted therapist or healer to guide you through the experience.

ZEBRA

POLARITY • INDIVIDUALITY • GROUP DYNAMICS • DEEPER EXPLORATION • EXPANSION

WHEN TO WORK WITH ME:

When you want to expand, when you don't want to be confined or boxed in, when you want to stand up for yourself in a healthy way, when you want to release victim mentality, when you want to be embraced for your uniqueness, when you want creative solutions to a problem

ENERGY MEDICINE:

One of my main medicines is powerful expression of individuality. If you fear losing your identity while in a relationship or group, reconnect to what makes you unique. Stand confident in who you truly are.

Do not let anyone put you in a box. Remember what you really want to achieve in life and do not limit yourself in order to make another person feel more comfortable.

Call upon me to show many solutions to any problem. I herald a time of change and expansion.

Stay true to your personal integrity and do not fall into victim mentality.

If you are drawn to me, you are ready to experience deeper layers within yourself and in your life. You know there is more than meets the eye. Call on me to guide you into other realms.

Cultivate healthier and more positive self-talk. Do not allow unfair or unhealthy criticisms to take space or energy in your mind or life.

POWER PRACTICE:

Every zebra has a unique striping pattern; no two zebras have the same coat. In this practice, you'll celebrate your unique qualities. First, close your eyes and visualize zebra with all its stripes. Call upon this powerful ally to work with you by saying, "Zebra, I invite you in now for this practice." Next, gently tap on your heart center, saying, "I honor my unique spirit." Then, with your journal and pen, write a list of the ten qualities you're proudest of, the stripes that make you who you are. Return to this list and ask zebra to work with you any time you need to be reminded of your unique beauty and power.

STRIPES FOR SURVIVAL

The zebra's stripes are important for their survival. When zebras are close together in a herd, the stripes of one zebra appear to merge with the stripes of another, making it hard for predators to discern which animal to target as prey.

THE BABOON AND THE ZEBRA

The San people of the Kalahari Desert in Namibia tell a story of how the zebra got its stripes. As the legend goes, when animals first came to this planet, the Earth was very hot and water was very limited. An old baboon sat by a fire and guarded one of the water holes. A white zebra (according to the tale, all zebras were white at this time) approached the hole, wanting a drink. The baboon proclaimed the zebra would have to fight him for the water. Zebra accepted the battle and in the course of the fight, kicked the baboon into the rocks behind them, then accidentally staggered into the fire, where he got scorched by the flames. It is said that the baboon got its hairless backside from being tossed onto the rocks, and the zebra got its black stripes from the fire.

ANIMAL POWER INDEX

FIND THE RIGHT ANIMAL FOR EVERY EXPERIENCE ON YOUR JOURNEY

BY EMOTION AND ENERGY

Using the list below, find the words that you want to call into your life. From there, you'll discover the animals that will help you manifest those qualities.

ABUNDANCE: Buffalo, Bull, Eagle, Ferret, Fly, Frog, Grasshopper, Koi, Pig, Rhinoceros, Squirrel, Stork, Swan, Turtle

ALIGNING WITH DIVINE TIMING: Alligator, Butterfly, Caterpillar, Chameleon, Praying Mantis, Raven, Rhinoceros, Squirrel, Turtle

ALIGNMENT: Ant, Giraffe

AUTHENTICITY: Black Jaguar, Condor, Peacock, Starfish, Zebra

BALANCE: Beaver, Bee, Bull, Chameleon, Condor, Flamingo, Giraffe, Kangaroo, Moose, Mountain Lion, Penguin, Pig, Roadrunner, Salamander, Shark, Squirrel, Wolf

BOUNDARIES: Armadillo, Skunk

CALM: Camel, Jellyfish, Koala, Llama, Pig, Stingray

CELEBRATION: Bee

CLARITY: Alligator, Caterpillar, Coyote, Cricket, Ferret, Fox, Giraffe, Penguin, Praying Mantis, Starfish, Worm

COMFORT: Bear, Black Jaguar

COMMITMENT: Camel, Eagle, Tiger

COMMUNITY: Ant, Beaver, Bee, Grasshopper, Kiwi, Monkey, Sheep, Snake, Vulture

COMPASSION: Elephant, Leopard, Sloth

CONFIDENCE AND SELF-ESTEEM: Ant, Bat, Bull, Chicken, Grasshopper, Leopard, Macaw, Moose, Mountain Goat, Rhinoceros, Seagull, Skunk, Squirrel, Swan, Wolf

CONNECTION: Beaver, Buffalo, Giraffe, Horse, Kiwi, Llama, Pig, Snake

COURAGE: Bear, Black Jaguar, Chicken, Cricket, Eagle, Frog, Grasshopper, Lion, Roadrunner

CREATIVITY: Bee, Bull, Caterpillar, Fox, Hippopotamus, Peacock, Seal, Snake, Spider, Whale

DETERMINATION AND PERSISTENCE: Ant, Beaver, Buffalo, Camel, Fly, Kangaroo, Koi, Leopard, Mountain Goat, Raccoon, Tiger, Wolf

DREAMS: Fox, Lizard, Penguin, Salamander

EASE: Beetle, Dolphin, Dragonfly, Giraffe, Koi, Octopus, Snail

ENERGETIC PROTECTION: Alligator, Armadillo, Condor, Ladybug, Llama, Mosquito, Owl, Roadrunner, Shark, Turtle

ENERGY: Bear, Buffalo, Dragonfly, Ferret, Tiger

EVOKING MAGIC AND MIRACLES: Alligator, Black Jaguar, Camel, Crow, Dolphin, Dragonfly, Hummingbird, Llama, Octopus, Raven, Rhinoceros

FERTILITY: Bee, Bull, Hippopotamus, Ostrich, Rabbit, Stork, Turtle, Vulture

FOCUS: Ant, Camel, Eagle, Giraffe, Hawk, Mouse, Roadrunner, Tiger

FORWARD MOVEMENT: Beaver, Beetle, Caterpillar, Fly, Frog, Horse, Kangaroo, Lizard, Roadrunner, Squirrel, Tiger

FREEDOM AND LIBERATION: Eagle, Horse

GOOD FORTUNE: Cricket, Grasshopper, Horse, Koi, Ladybug, Pig

GRATITUDE: Buffalo, Dolphin, Lizard, Sheep

GROUNDEDNESS: Bear, Camel, Ferret, Kangaroo, Kiwi, Ostrich, Stork, Turtle, Worm

HEALING: Dragonfly, Ferret, Frog, Manatee, Mouse, Octopus, Raccoon, Tiger, Worm

HEALTHY BOUNDARIES: Armadillo, Eagle, Lizard, Mountain Lion, Skunk

HIGH VISION: Bee, Eagle, Giraffe, Hawk, Kangaroo, Mountain Goat

HUMOR: Duck, Fox, Rooster

INDEPENDENCE: Armadillo, Eagle, Leopard, Mountain Goat, Octopus, Seagull, Wolf

SPIRITUAL GIFTS: Alligator, Beetle, Camel, Chameleon, Chicken, Condor, Cricket, Dolphin, Dragonfly, Duck, Giraffe, Octopus, Owl, Raccoon, Raven, Snail, Spider, Vulture, Whale

STRENGTH: Bear, Bull, Camel, Deer, Eagle, Hippopotamus, Koi, Komodo Dragon, Mountain Lion, Penguin, Tiger

SURRENDER: Chameleon, Horse, Lizard, Octopus, Praying Mantis, Swan, Turtle

TEAMWORK: Ant, Beaver

TRANSITION, CHANGE, AND TRANSFORMATION: Bat, Beetle, Black Jaguar, Butterfly, Caterpillar, Chameleon, Crab, Crow, Frog, Lizard, Mosquito, Raccoon, Raven, Salamander

TRUST: Ant, Bat, Bear, Black Jaguar, Camel, Dragonfly, Koala, Porcupine, Roadrunner, Seal, Squirrel

TRUTH: Alligator, Caterpillar, Chameleon, Chicken, Condor, Dragonfly, Duck, Ferret, Hawk, Jellyfish, Kiwi, Llama, Owl, Raccoon

WISDOM: Eagle, Giraffe, Hawk, Heron, Jellyfish, Mountain Lion, Owl, Octopus, Raven, Tiger, Turtle, Whale

BY ANIMAL

In this section, you can find information on the energy medicine of every animal in the book.

ALLIGATOR

When you are ready to let yourself see truth, when you want clarity on whether to pause or act, when you want to further develop your spiritual gifts and abilities, when you want to evoke magic and miracles

ANT

When you want to get into alignment with your goals and dreams, when you're ready to do what's needed to serve the greater good, when you need more patience and trust, when you want to hone in on a clear strategy, when you're working with a team or community

ARMADILLO

When you want to establish healthy boundaries, when you want to claim independence, when you want to respect yourself and be respected by others, when you want to heal people-pleasing tendencies, when you want to stay in your power

BAT

When you're moving through big life transitions, when you're facing your darkest fears, when your soul knows it's time to go deeper inward than ever before, when you're ready to place the greatest trust in self and the Universe

BEAR

When you need to be energetically recharged, when you need comfort, when you want to feel held by the love of the universe, when you want to learn to go within and trust yourself, when you want to feel more grounded, when you need to stand in your power

BEAVER

When you want to build something strong, when you want healthy relationships and team dynamics, when you want to go after your dreams, when you want a happy home, when you want to balance work and play, when you want to get out of your own way

BEE

When you're ready to achieve the "impossible," when you want to tap into your royal roots, when you want to deeply connect with true community and family, when you're ready to "pollinate" special projects and relationships

BEETLE

When you want to be more optimistic, when you're going through major change or rebirth, when you are ready for spiritual advancement, when you're ready to embody your full power, when you're ready to bring forward new life, when you want more ease, when you want to get through hard times with grace

BLACK JAGUAR

When you're going through uncertainty and change, when you're ready to do shadow work, when working with the moon, when you're ready for a complete rebirth, when you're ready to reclaim your power

BUFFALO

When you need to reconnect with gratitude and abundance, when you're feeling strong and want to support others in need, when you want to be sure you're on the best track, when you want to manifest your highest good

BULL

When you need immense strength, when you want to be a better leader, when you want to have a baby, when you want more abundance, when you want balanced masculine and feminine energies, when you don't want to be stubborn or operate from ego, when you want steadfast belief in working toward a goal

BUTTERFLY

When you're ready to evolve with joy, when you want to be filled with lightheartedness, when you're ready to get in sync with the energy of the Universe, when you're ready to accept that the magic of life is right here, right now

CAMEL

When you are going through a tough time in life, when you feel like giving up, when you need reminding of your strength, when you need power to continue, when you're in harsh environments or situations, when you feel alone

CATERPILLAR

When you need to remember you're exactly where you're meant to be, when you need new inspiration and ideas, when you need clarity before making a decision, when you're ready for the next phase of life

CHAMELEON

When you need your energy to be balanced, when you want to embrace change, when you want to embody your full power, when you want to open your supernatural abilities, when you want stronger intuition, when you want to see truth, when you want a better game plan

CHICKEN

When you want to speak with confidence, when you want to step out into the world bravely, when you want to move your body freely, when you want to see through people's intentions and energies, when you want to expand into a life of service

CLAM

When you're ready to stop hiding your talents and gifts, when you want to invite more happiness, when you're ready to put in the inner work to experience true freedom, when you're ready to transcend fears that have held you back, when you're ready to take responsibility for your life

CONDOR

When you are ready to see truth, when you are ready to awaken spiritually, when you are ready to activate your feminine power, when you are ready to expand past confines, when you're ready to transcend limiting patterns and fears, when you're ready for more freedom

COYOTE

When you want to see through illusion, when you want to drop the mask you've been wearing, when you're ready for truth to be revealed, when you're ready to let go of victim mentality

CRAB

When you need to move past an obstacle, when you're ready to let love in, when you want to revamp your home, when you want to embrace your sensitivities and emotions more, when you're ready to satiate curiosities, when you're ready to explore and transform

CRICKET

When you want to seize big opportunities, when you want to express your soul's purpose, when you want to open your heart, when you need clarity on decisions, when you want to be filled with integrity, when you want high vibrations

CROW

When you are ready to trust your personal integrity, when you want to align with your power during times of great change or uncertainty, when you are ready to birth a new project or way of living, when you need spiritual strength

DEER

When you want your heart to heal or open, when you want to inspire through kindness rather than force, when you want to give and receive unconditional love, when you want to stop being so hard on yourself or others.

DOLPHIN

When you want to clear old emotions, when you want to be more playful, when you want to communicate, when you want to connect with your mystical gifts, when you want to activate your intelligence, when you want to experience greater ease, when you want to access the ancient wisdoms inside of you

DRAGONFLY

When you want more ease and grace in your life, when you're ready for a swift change and don't want to resist it, when you want to break free of old patterns holding you back, when you want to shift past an old mentality or way of thinking, when you're ready to release suffering and activate more lightheartedness into your life

DUCK

When you want to connect with your emotions, when you want to step into your spiritual gifts, when you want to lead or teach, when you don't want to get pulled into other people's drama, when you want to call forward sacred partnership, when you want to be more playful

EAGLE

When you need a healthier or broader perspective, when you want more freedom and independence, when you want to get in touch with your sexuality, when you want to practice nonattachment, when you want to see through falsehoods and have effective communication

ELEPHANT

When you want to connect with family, when you want to unlock your ancient wisdom, when you want to be more likable, when you want to be more adventurous sexually, when you want to remove blocks, when you want more self-honor

FERRET

When you're involved in negotiations, when you need to sniff out truths, when you need to restore, when you want abundant supplies, when you're ready to take responsibility, when you want to process surprising information, when you need to be reminded that all is sacred

FLAMINGO

When you need to find balance, when you need to let loose, when you need to spend time with or appreciate your friends and family more, when you need an emotional healing or clearing, when you want to open your heart

FLY

When you need to complete a project or goal, when you need to release victim mentality, when you need to turn hardship into gold, when you need to find the path of least resistance, when you need to clear your life of negativity

FOX

When you need clever solutions or smart ideas, when you need clear insight before making a decision, when you want to properly assess your surroundings and relationships, when you need more humor in your life, when you want to understand messages in your dreams

FROG

When you're in need of emotional healing, when you're working with the element of water, when you need courage to move forward, when you want to allow in more wealth, when you want to open to new possibilities

GIRAFFE

When you're ready to get unstuck or overcome whatever is holding you back, when you want to stop worrying, when you want to improve your personal relationships, when you want support to reach your highest dreams

GNAT

When you want to shake irritability, when you want a shift in perspective, when you want to embody your full power, when you want to feel empowered during trying times, when you want to get to the bottom of a lesson

GRASSHOPPER

When you want to activate more abundance in your life, when you need a dose of courage to take the leap, when you're ready to make a change in your career, when you want to confidently use your voice, when you want to bring a group together for a positive purpose

HAWK

When you are tired of dimming your inner light, when you're ready to take steps to align your life with your soul's purpose on Earth, when you need to stay focused, when you want relief, when you want to activate psychic abilities

HERON

When you want to access unseen realms, when you want to open to your mystic wisdom, when you want to have the fullest life experience possible, when you want to connect with your breath, when you're ready for deep contemplation

HIPPOPOTAMUS

When you're ready to deal with your emotions in a healthy way, when you want to be unaffected by other people's words, when you want to connect to parental powers and instincts, when you want to birth something new, when you want to work with the element of water

HORSE

When you want to feel free, when you want to break through limitations, when you want to unleash your full power, when you want to experience loyalty and devotion, when you are ready to embark on new adventures, when you want to have healthy sexual experiences

HUMMINGBIRD

When you want to awaken more joy, when you want to be present to life's miracles, when you want to see beauty everywhere, when you want to release feelings of bitterness or resentment, when you want to have a happy home, when you need to be reminded you live in a world of infinite possibilities

JELLYFISH

When you want to feel and express your emotions in a healthy way, when you want direct access to the trust and wisdom of the Universe, when you want to connect more deeply with your heart, when you want to flow but not drift aimlessly

KANGAROO

When you want to move forward, when you want stability and balance in your life, when you want to honor Great Mother Earth, when you want to show true kindness toward children and animals, when you want to eliminate or move past distractions

KIWI

When you want to discern honesty from dishonesty, when you want to work more deeply with Earth medicine, when you want more sweetness in your life, when you want to bring people and causes together, when you want to spend more time in the forest

KOALA

When you want to slow down and relax, when you want to release anger, when you want to open up paternal instincts, when you want to be less reactive, when you want to release addiction to drama or stress, when you want to forgive, when you want to let go of grudges and animosity, when you want to experience awe, when you want to trust the big picture

KOI

When you need more peace and calm, when you want to have a stronger meditative practice, when you want to connect with your ancestors, when you want to appreciate or invite in meaningful friendships, when you want financial success and wealth

KOMODO DRAGON

When you need to be stronger than ever before, when you want to summon a powerful new energy within you, when you need to take swift and decisive action, when you need to stand strong in the face of others people's opinions, when you need to step boldly into a new life, when you need to exit a toxic situation

LADYBUG

When you want to experience more joy and good fortune, when you need energetic protection, when you want to activate higher consciousness, when you want to connect to the power of the present moment

LEECH

When you want to feel reinvigorated and strong, when you want to release judgments or fears, when you want to remove toxicity, when you want your life to head in a new direction, when you want more trust, when you're going through a big transition

LEOPARD

When you're ready to embrace what makes you unique, when you want to deepen your spiritual gifts, when you need to build self-confidence, when you're ready to release ego, when you're stepping into a leadership role

LION

When you want to act from a place of honesty and integrity, when you need more courage, when you want to be a respected leader, when you're ready to approach life with vigor and passion, when you want healthy new friendships, when you want to be more generous

LIZARD

When you are ready to initiate change in your life, when you are ready to let go of what you've clung to in the past, when you want to transcend fear, when you need support moving forward, when you want to understand and act upon messages in your dreams

LLAMA

When you want to feel a sense of connection, when you want to experience serenity, when you want to express yourself truthfully, when you want support, when you need more fun in your life, when you want your business or career to be infused with spirituality

MACAW

When you want to use the power of your voice, when you're ready to meet your sacred partner, when you want to connect with the power of the sun, when you want to bring positive energy to the world, when you want to be more extroverted, when you're done feeling like you're "too much," when you want to proudly express your uniqueness

MANATEE

When your heart needs healing, when you want to be more trusting of yourself and others, when you want to evoke ancient wisdom, when you want to awaken your intuition, when you want to experience gentle love and soothing peace

MONKEY

When you want to get along with a group, when you're ready to lead, when you're moving into a new home or making a big change, when you want to be more playful and fun, when you need to make fast and clear decisions, when you want to take on more responsibility or leadership

MOOSE

When you want to enhance your self-esteem and self-honor, when you want to heal from childhood wounds, when you want to operate from a place of deep wisdom, when you want to explore your metaphysical depths and abilities

MOSQUITO

When you want power over your emotions and small annoyances, when you want to clear energy suckers from your life, when you want to skillfully navigate big change, when you want a positive attitude and mindset, when you want to stop taking things too seriously

MOTH

When you want to realize what you need to let go of, when you're ready for closure, when you want to transform shadow energy or clear your energy field, when you want to remain optimistic, when you want to move toward what is positive for you and your life

MOUNTAIN GOAT

When you want to reach a lofty goal with a strong foundation and confidence, when you want to get out of a rut, when you want to strengthen your determination and ambition, when you want to have healthy sexual relations, when you're ready to break out of your comfort zone

MOUNTAIN LION

When you need to be empowered as a leader, when you're ready to actualize a goal using higher wisdom, when you want extra protection and strength, when you need to soothe your anxieties, when you need to balance mind, body, spirit, and soul

MOUSE

When you need to focus, when it's time to get out of survival mode, when you need to think outside the box, when you want to let go of old stories and emotions, when you want to release stress, when you want to reconnect to your power

OCTOPUS

When you need to multitask, when you want to experience life with more grace and ease, when you need to heal something, when you need to loosen up, when you want to be alluring, when you're ready to be independent, when you want to connect to the mystical dance of the universe

OSTRICH

When you need to be present, when you need protection from drama or stress, when want to call more fertility into your life, when you want to feel grounded, when you want to apply cosmic knowledge in your daily life, when you want to raise your frequency and consciousness, when you want to process something big

OWL

When you need to see through deception, when you want to see beyond people's masks, when you're ready to face illusions and shadows, when you want to awaken your seer abilities, when you're experiencing a death and rebirth, when you want to do shadow work, when you want to awaken esoteric wisdom

PEACOCK

When you're ready to cultivate self-love, when you want creative inspiration, when you're ready to shine bright, when you're ready to open your third eye, when you're ready for creative inspiration, when you're ready for your rebirth

PENGUIN

When you are looking for a monogamous relationship, when you need balance in life, when you want to receive messages in your dreams, when you need strength to make sacrifices, when you want to be respected or give more respect, when you need a dose of optimism

PIG

When you want to attract sincere people, when you want to be more generous, when you want steady financial wealth, when you want to have a foundation of abundance, when you want a balance between relaxation and passion, when you want to clear scarcity mentality, when you want to be unaffected by the opinions of others

PORCUPINE

When you need a break from the stresses of adulthood, when you want to reconnect to the joys of childhood, when you want to connect with your ancestors, when you want to take care of your body and eat well, when you want to let your defenses down, when you want to trust again

PRAYING MANTIS

When you need to make wise choices, when you want to act with precision, when you want to deepen your mindfulness practice, when you need more patience, when you want to slow down and connect with inner wisdom, when you want to sharpen your clairvoyant abilities, when you want to do the greatest good

RABBIT

When you want to seize an opportunity, when you want to activate a new life force, when you are entering a committed relationship, when you want to work with the cycles and power of the moon, when you're ready to face your fears, when you want to release stress

RACCOON

When you want permission to change, when you want to see playful new options, when you want to awaken your healing abilities, when you want fierce determination to reach your goal, when you want to see through secrets or lies, when you want to be helpful

RAVEN

When you want to be a better communicator, when you want to be in sacred alignment with the Universe, when you're ready to face darkness so that you can experience light, when you're ready for a shift in consciousness when you want fresh energy, when you're ready to clear debris in your life, when you want to experience passion, when you want clear solutions, when you want confidence as you expand and grow

RHINOCEROS

When you want to blast through obstacles and level up (especially in your career), when you want to release procrastination, when you want more enlightenment in your life, when you want to be a magnet for abundance, when you need to be reminded that life is full of miracles

ROADRUNNER

When you want to stop procrastinating, when you want to change the energy within you or a room, when you want to make quick decisions with clarity, when you want mental strength, when you need to trust your gut, when you feel overwhelmed

ROOSTER

When you want supportive relationships, when you need to get in touch with your magnificence, when you want to expand your joy, when you want more ease and humor in your life, when you want clarity on intentions (yours and others'), when you want to have healthy relationships

SALAMANDER

When you want to maintain a healthy mindset during a period of change, when you're ready to experience reverence and trust toward your emotions, when you're ready to break free of a pattern, when you want to burn away old aspects holding you back, when you want to embrace transformation

SEAGULL

When you want respect, when you don't want to settle for less than you deserve,

SEAL

When you want to improve your relationships, when you want to trust yourself to feel deeply, when you want to connect with chanting or song, when you want to open your imagination and creativity, when you want to heal a maternal relationship, when you want to hear your inner wisdom, when you want to awaken to the oneness of all that is

SHARK

When you need to navigate your fears, when you're ready to clear negative people or energy, when you want to have better work-life balance, when you want to be in tune with your emotions and communicate in a healthy way, when you want to be a pro at navigating life's journey

SHEEP

When you want to act with an open heart, when you want to be awake to the world around you, when you want to bring people together, when you want to focus on global harmony, when you want to feel more gratitude, when you want to be less afraid, when you want to remain optimistic

SKUNK

When you want respect, when you want to cultivate self-love, when you want to heighten sexual relationships, when you need to draw clear boundaries, when you want to insulate yourself from criticism and judgments

SLOTH

When you want to release being judgmental, when you want to be more open-minded, when you need a boost to keep going, when you want to be present and enjoy life, when you need to be methodical

SNAIL

When you want to find a way to work that is not too fast or stressful, when you want to break out of your comfort zone, when you want to choose the easiest path, when you want to reconsider the pace of a relationship

SNAKE

When you are ready to let go of what no longer serves you, when you want to set yourself free, when you are ready to awaken your true spiritual life force from within, when you want to align with your divine sexual and creative powers

SPIDER

When embarking on a new phase of life, when you desire harmony, when you want to activate more magic in your life, when you want to transcend fear, when you want to approach things with curiosity, when you're ready to move forward with intention

SQUIRREL

When you need more play in your life, when you want the security of ample resources, when you want to declutter, when you want to trust the cycles of movement and rest, when you want confidence to take action

STARFISH

When you want to experience infinite love, when you're in need of clarity, when you're ready to embrace your unique soul purpose, when you want to stabilize your emotions, when you want to forge ahead regardless of what others say, when you want to be more generous

STINGRAY

When you want time to yourself, when you need a break, when you want to avoid drama or conflict, when you want to get to the root of healing emotional patterns, when you want support in knowing how to pick and choose battles, when you do not want to react from emotions

STORK

When you want to heal childhood or ancestral wounds, when you want to birth something new, when you want to have healthy roots and a stable home, when you want to connect with other realms, when you're ready to have good fortune and prosperity

SWAN

When you want a sacred partnership, when you are ready for more wealth, when you want to access your intuitive powers, when you want to embody more grace and beauty, when you want to be more comfortable in a group

TICK

When you want to practice nonattachment, when you want to embody your full power, when you want to transcend your fears, when you don't want to ignore what's holding you back anymore, when you want to alchemize and heal trauma

TIGER

When you want to awaken sensuality and passion, when you want to grow stronger with each lesson in life, when you want strong focus, when you're ready for new adventures, when you need energy, when you want to be a great leader

TURTLE

When you need to feel protected, when you want to feel more grounded, when you want to connect with the Earth, when you're ready to tune in to ancient wisdom, when you need endurance, when you want to invite abundance and fertility

VULTURE

When you want to be in a healthy community, when you want more kindness in your life, when you want to be purified, when you want to open abilities to read auras, when you want to open your clairvoyant gifts, when you don't want to feel lost or alone anymore, when you want to rise from hard times better than ever

WALRUS

When you want to gain deeper knowledge, when you need to embody parental love, when you need affection, when you want to be more sociable, when you want to host a gathering, when you want to see more beauty in the world

WHALE

When you want to tap into more spiritual energies, when you want to work with sound and song, when you want a boost in life, when you need to communicate better, when you want to stay in your power, when you want to connect to Great Mother Earth

WOLF

When you want to strike a balance between being independent and social, when you want to be the best teacher you can be, when you want to embody strong family values, when you want to connect to nature, when you need self-confidence, when you want to align with the powers of the moon

WORM

When you want to feel fulfilled, when you want to connect with the Earth, when you want to see what needs to be healed from your past, when you want to improve your environment

ZEBRA

When you want to expand, when you don't want to be confined or boxed in, when you want to stand up for yourself in a healthy way, when you want to release victim mentality, when you want to be embraced for your uniqueness, when you want creative solutions to a problem

RESOURCES AND ADVOCACY

SUPPORTING INDIGENOUS COMMUNITIES AND PROTECTING ANIMALS AND NATURAL RESOURCES

SUPPORT FOR INDIGENOUS AND FIRST NATION COMMUNITIES

It is vital that we all do our part to preserve ancient and sacred lands, cultures, and wisdoms. The following organizations support First Nations and Indigenous communities:

Aniwa

Aniwa is a movement that invites all peoples to join together to initiate positive change, unity, and harmony for the planet. Their main mission is to amplify Indigenous wisdom. Aniwa activates these goals through ancient ceremonies, cultural exchange, and more. Aniwa gatherings are nonprofit events that bring many of the world's most respected Indigenous leaders together to share their traditions. You can support them at www.aniwa.co.

Amazon Front Lines

Amazon Front Lines defends Indigenous rights to land and life and works to preserve the culture in the Amazon rainforest. To learn more, visit www.amazonfrontlines.org

Amazon Watch

Amazon Watch works on climate change, protecting the rainforest, and supporting Indigenous rights. To learn more, visit amazonwatch.org

The Bavubuka Foundation

The Bavubuka Foundation is dedicated to creating spaces and educational programs that nurture and empower a new generation of young leaders in Uganda and all of Africa to use their voices to communicate positive messages and affect positive change in their communities and the world. Each Bavubuka project incorporates reconciliation and peace-building activities by using transformative art to cultivate personal empowerment within a united communal effort.

The BOA Foundation

The BOA Foundation is a nonprofit organization that focuses on supporting Indigenous communities and the preservation of sacred land, cultures, and ancient wisdom. Many of their initiatives include land buy-back, sustainable living solutions, and ecosystem restoration. To learn more, visit www.theboafoundation.org.

The Cultural Conservancy

This group collaborates with a range of communities and organizations in the Americas and Pacific to revitalize Native cultures and their ancestral lands. To learn more, visit www.nativeland.org

Dig Deep

Dig Deep works on getting running water across Navajo Nation in the United States and supports water being delivered to other communities in need. To learn more, visit www.digdeep.org

Descendants of the Earth

This organization works on the preservation of the traditions and values of Native American culture. To learn more, visit www.descendantsoftheearth.org

If Not Us Then Who

This organization supports Indigenous peoples in protecting the planet and empowering them to bring about positive social change. To learn more, visit ifnotusthenwho.me/about/

International Indigenous Youth Council

This organization supports education, civic engagement, and spiritual practices for indigenous youth throughout the world. To learn more, visit indigenousyouth.org.

Naku

This organization works to preserve the Sapara traditions of the Ecuadorian Amazon and foster a better education system for Sapara children. To learn more, visit www.naku.com.ec.

Pacha Mama

This organization applies Indigenous wisdom rooted in the Amazon rainforest and supports environmental sustainability, social justice, and spiritual presence. Learn more by visiting www.pachamama.org.

Pueblo Relief Fund

The Pueblo Relief Fund supports the needs of the Pueblo Nations. Learn more by visiting pueblorelieffund.org.

Soul of the Mother

Soul of the Mother was founded to restore ancient Indigenous wisdom, heal Great Mother Earth, and support the spiritual evolution of humanity. To learn more, visit www.soulofthemother.org.

Root to Heaven

This organization works directly with Indigenous elders and nations on ecological projects that support reforestation, rehabilitation, and regeneration. To learn more, visit www.roottoheaven.com.

SUPPORT FOR ANIMALS AND NATURAL RESOURCES

The following organizations work to maintain heathy animal populations and protect and restore natural habitats.

Amboseli Trust for Elephants

This trust works on protecting elephants in Africa through advocacy, scientific research, and community outreach. To learn more, visit www.elephanttrust.org.

Buffalo Field Campaign

Buffalo are endangered. There are only 20,000 left in North America, down from 50 to 80 million. To learn more, visit www.buffalofieldcampaign.org.

Earth Alliance

This organization is committed to preserving Earth's biodiversity and addressing urgent threats to the planet. To learn more, visit: ealliance.org.

Earth Justice

According to earthjustice.org, nearly one-third of all honeybees in the United States have died in the last few years. Scientists don't know the exact cause, but a growing body of independent data links a class of pesticides called neonicotinoids (neonics) to widespread bee die-offs, both alone and in combination with other factors like disease and malnutrition. Twenty-nine independent scientists conducted a global review of 800 independent studies and found overwhelming evidence of pesticides linked to bee declines. Earthjustice represents a coalition of food safety and environmental health groups in a case against the state of California's Department of Pesticide Regulation for its approval of neonicotinoid pesticides and failure to study the science around harm to bees. According to environmental horticulturalist Laura Anne Sanagorski, less than 5 percent of the world's insects are harmful to humans or crops, meaning that 95 percent of insects killed by blanket applications of pesticides are not pests and may even be beneficial. To learn more, visit earthjustice.org.

Jaguar Rescue Center

This foundation helps rehabilitate injured, sick, or orphaned animals and release them back into the wild, and to preserve natural ecosystems and native wildlife. To learn more, visit www.jaguarrescue.foundation.

The Jane Goodall Institute

This institute has a wide range of initiatives to protect chimpanzees and other great apes, promote healthy habitats, and help address conservation challenges. To learn more, visit www.janegoodall.org.

Jungle Keepers

This organization works to protect the world's rainforests. To learn more, visit www.junglekeepers.com.

LeCiel Foundation

This foundation funds land and cultural preservation, helps humans reconnect with the natural world, and promotes holistic solutions for global change. To learn more, visit lecielfoundation.com.

The Leilani Farm Sanctuary

This farm sanctuary in Hawai'i saves and cares for animals who are orphaned or destined for slaughter. To learn more, visit leilanifarmsanctuary.org.

Loveland Farm Sanctuary

This sanctuary helps abused or neglected farm animals. To learn more, visit: www.lovelandfarmsanctuary.org

Ol Pejeta Conservancy

After years of widespread poaching and civil war in its home range devastated its population, the northern white rhino is now considered extinct in the wild and there are only two left on the planet, both located at the Ol Pejeta Conservancy in Kenya. The great news is that we can help save this subspecies from extinction. The future of the northern white rhino now lies in the development of in vitro fertilization techniques and stem cell technology, costly and complicated procedures that have never before been attempted in rhinos. You can support Ol Pejeta Conservancy at donate.olpejetaconservancy.org.

American Wild Horse Campaign

This organization works to protect wild horses and burros throughout the United States. To learn more, visit americanwildhorsecampaign.org.

One Tree Planted

This organization works on reforestation and biodiversity through their initiative to plant trees all over the world. To learn more, visit onetreeplanted.org

Polar Bears International

This organization works to protect polar bears and their habitats. To learn more, visit polarbearsinternational.org

Roatan Rescue

This organization supports the rescue and rehabilitation of abused or neglected animals in Honduras. To learn more, visit www.roatanrescue.com.

Sea Shepherd Conservation Society

Sea Shepherd works to protect marine wildlife worldwide. To learn more, visit seashepherd.org.

Sheldrick Wildlife Trust

This trust works to protect and preserve Africa's threatened wildlife and habitats. To learn more, visit, www.sheldrickwildlifetrust.org.

Wild Screen

This organization brings conservationists together with leading photographers, filmmakers, and other creatives to create stories about the natural world in order to inspire a wide audience to care for the environment. To learn more, visit ww.wildscreen.org.

The Wolf Conservation Center

This organization works to protect wolves in North America and teach people about wolves. To learn more, visit nywolf.org.

ACKNOWLEDGMENTS

Where do I even begin? So many countless miracles have occurred for me to have gotten here, to this point in my life, where I am writing this page in my book. I most deeply revere and acknowledge it all. Thank you to every breath, every soul whisper, every blade of grass, every emotion, every realization, every footstep, every dream, every human I've crossed paths with. I thank the totality of this existence and all of my other existences, because every drop of it has brought me here to this most glorious place where I get to write a book in collaboration with one hundred miraculous animals.

Thank you for caring about this planet, your own personal evolution, and other living beings, and for honoring this life. It truly is the honoring of life that is most important, because it is all sacred—every bit of it. As you continue on your spiritual or shamanic path, regularly reflect upon and honor the places you connect with most to receive your guidance. It is also important to pay homage in various ways to the First Peoples of this planet, as many of them who are spiritual elders have taken sacred oaths and come from unbroken lineages of family members completely devoted to preserving the most ancient spiritual truths of this planet. Many have worked tirelessly and very bravely to do so. It is also very important to pay homage in various ways to Great Mother Earth, Great Spirit, the elements, the sun, the moon, and, of course, your own being—mind, body, spirit, and soul. Honor and thank your own heart for its willingness to stay open and lead the way. And remember, you are always the best guide for you when you are connected to your soul, your highest self, and the Divine.

Blessings always, Alyson Charles

To Willian,

From the first moment I saw your unique, vibrant, and expressive art, I knew you were the artist who could create illustrations to embody the full healing attributes of each magical animal. This book has been the biggest labor of love for my career thus far, and I could not have had it come together so powerfully without you. I am incredibly happy and honored to have been able to collaborate with you. We were able to create a breathtakingly beautiful book and also do our part in activating an even bigger mission: the Eagle and Condor Prophecy. Your energies from the South uniting and working with my energies from the North played a divine role in ushering in a time of higher consciousness and unity for the world. I promise to always do my best to hold the strongest container to allow the energy of your magnificent art to reach as many hearts as possible. May your spirit and legacy live on in the most divine ways, always.

Blessings, Alyson